ANIMATION SKETCHBOOKS

ANIMATION SKETCHBOOKS

LAURA HEIT

Thames & Hudson

CONTENTS

Laura Heit is an award-winning animator and puppeteer based in Portland, Oregon. See page 87 for a full biography.

For Kris and Leo Dallas

Front cover: sketchbook drawing by Malcolm Sutherland
Back cover: sketchbook drawing by Mirai Mizue

page 2: Isabel Herguera
page 6: photograph of Priit Pärn © Olga Pärn
page 7: photograph of Jim Trainor © Caroline Nutley
page 8: Osbert Parker

First published in the United Kingdom in 2013 by
Thames & Hudson Ltd, 181A High Holborn, London WC1V 7QX

Animation Sketchbooks © 2013 Thames & Hudson Ltd, London

Individual illustrations © 2013 the artists or as detailed
on page 319

Text © 2013 Laura Heit

ISBN 978-0-500-51675-1

Printed and bound in China by C&C Offset Printing Co Ltd

To find out about all our publications, please visit
www.thamesandhudson.com. There you can subscribe
to our e-newsletter, browse or download our current
catalogue, and buy any titles that are in print.

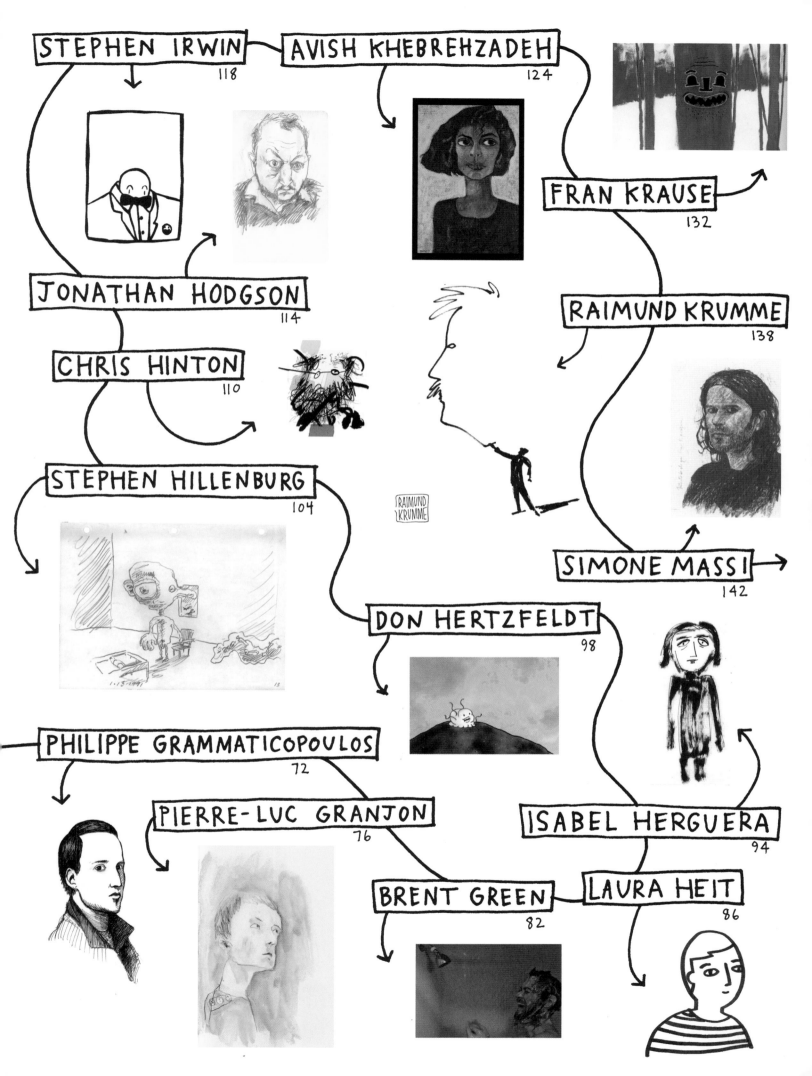

STEPHEN IRWIN 118

AVISH KHEBREHZADEH 124

FRAN KRAUSE 132

JONATHAN HODGSON 114

RAIMUND KRUMME 138

CHRIS HINTON 110

RAIMUND KRUMME

STEPHEN HILLENBURG 104

SIMONE MASSI 142

DON HERTZFELDT 98

PHILIPPE GRAMMATICOPOULOS 72

PIERRE-LUC GRANJON 76

ISABEL HERGUERA 94

BRENT GREEN 82

LAURA HEIT 86

DAVID OREILLY
166

OSBERT PARKER
172

PRIIT PÄRN
178

MIRAI MIZUE
160

MICHAELA PAVLÁTOVÁ
186

REGINA PESSOA
194

MAUREEN SELWOOD
224

FLORENCE MIAILHE
154

MIWA MATREYEK
148

GEORGES SCHWIZGEBEL
218

DAVID POLONSKY
200

JEFF SCHER
206

ALLISON SCHULNIK
212

TOKYO SPA
MEN & WOMEN

SCHWIZGEBEL

INTRODUCTION

I have been a sketchbook peeper whenever the opportunity has presented itself. Mostly closed to viewers, with only the occasional over-the-shoulder peek, or a lucky look between friends or collaborators, the pages within a sketchbook remain loosely, sometimes fiercely, guarded. A sketchbook affords the mark-maker a safe place to play, to experiment, and to be unusually free. It is here that drawing can become wholly uninhibited, unencumbered by critique or criticism. This book opens these often un-public sketchbooks and offers us a unique chance to espy ideas as they appear in their infancy, a film in its first stirrings, an animator's drawings made when they are not animating. There are no mistakes here, just first gestures, unselfconscious sketches, odd bits glued on, lists, notes, scribbles, jottings, and doodles. An exclusive unveiling of the beauty, sincerity, and mania of the animator's intimate process, this book's purpose is to offer insight and inspiration, incite creative possibility, and compel you to draw and, perhaps, to make films.

And what joy! To my surprise, almost everyone I invited to submit his or her sketchbooks was immediately interested. A common response was: "I can't wait to see other people's work!" Collecting the images for this book was like receiving presents— I'd get an email saying an artist's images were

uploaded and I would eagerly open the folders, never disappointed with their contents. It was no easy task choosing the artists for this book—there were some I could not find, some who only work on the computer these days, some who said their drawings were terrible, and I could not convince them otherwise, and some who were too busy making films to participate. What you will see are over 50 animation artists from all over the world, representing a huge range of animation styles and techniques. I invited those whose work I have long admired and who are internationally recognized, and a few whose work is just being discovered. I chose artists who have made work recently, and whose work fits into an independent spirit of filmmaking, with art as the basis of the work. They may work commercially for a living, but this is not the work the book showcases. There was one rule: the images submitted must have been created on PAPER. This sounds redundant since this is a book about sketchbooks, but filmmakers are deep into, and mostly on the other side of, a transition into working digitally. Animators often work on the computer now, making early sketches and designs using a tablet and stylus. Some of those I approached hardly draw on paper at all any more and regretfully declined to be included. As the majority of films are produced using software and

1

2

3

digital processes, this book can be viewed as a document of a field in transition, a reference to a previous tradition of filmmaking. At the same time, I believe the sketchbook has made a comeback of sorts, as artists have become weary of endless hours in front of a computer, and grow nostalgic for the time when they simply took out a pencil and began to draw. Animation is a long and often tedious process, so for an animator a sketchbook can be a place to put down thoughts quickly. If the rest of your art practice is repetitive and time intensive then the process of drawing can in itself be liberating.

You will discover many types of sketchbook keepers within these pages. You will find early ideas plotted out, sometimes repeatedly until their purpose becomes clear, thumbnail sketches of developing characters, mini storyboards scratched out in a hurry. There are those who try out new mark-making techniques, searching for the next film's look. Others use the pages to doodle mindlessly as a kind of artistic respite, their work here unrelated to their film projects. Some keep a book like a travelogue, carrying it with them on all of their adventures. Isabel Herguera took hers to India and came back with so many rich and vivid drawings they became the basis for her film *Ámár* (2010, fig. 1). Others, such as Luis Cook, treat their sketchbook

like a reliquary, part scrapbook, part personal project (fig. 2). There are examples of guides written for the artist alone—they look pragmatic or nondescript, nothing like their finished, often remarkably rendered films. Avish Khebrehzadeh draws large horizontal maps of her film projects, plotting images against sounds in a landscape of pencil marks and marginalia. Don Hertzfeldt gives us camera notes, explaining that they are his own coded notations for complex 35 mm camera moves and double exposures (fig. 5). Many storyboard in their sketchbooks, plotting early ideas for scenes or hastily sketching out solutions for a film that needs rethinking (figs 3 and 4). Other artists show us how they work out the smallest of actions: an over-the-shoulder glance, a bear scratching his nose, pages filled with tiny figures in various poses, a face drawn from 20 angles, an astronaut seen from 14 points of view, each drawing a kind of audition. Quick, spontaneous sketches often have the energy subsequently sought after, as the figure becomes a character to be drawn frame by frame (figs 6, 7 and 8). While more uncommon, some have the inclination to make their sketchbooks public. Animator Fran Krause made his entire film *Nosy Bear* (2011) on the pages of his sketchbook, and regularly posts these pages on his blog. Then there are the animators who do not draw: they use collage as a

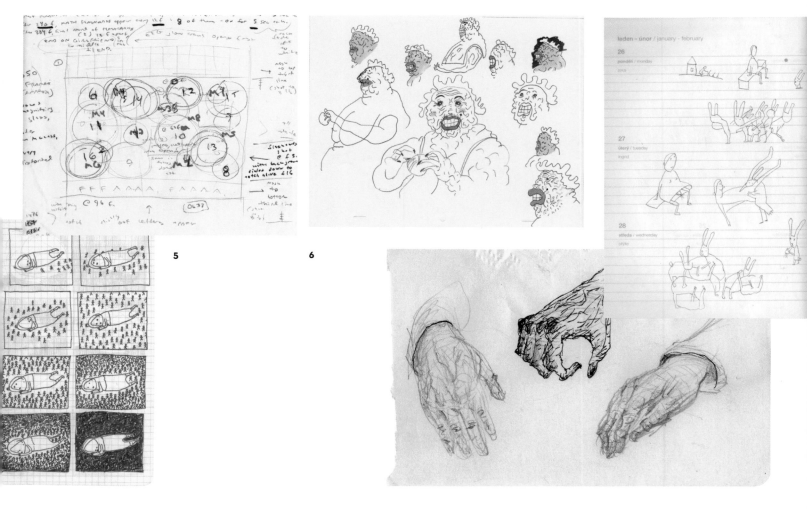

5

6

form of image making. Martha Colburn researches a subject and collages hundreds of images with cut-out puppets, incorporating magazine pages, printed Google image searches, lost and found detritus, bits of painted acetate and puzzle pieces (fig. 9). David OReilly works in 3D CGI and doesn't keep a sketchbook anymore. He sent me the only thing he still does on paper: "to-do lists," each one a document of a day's work on his films. Details such as "eat lunch" tell us how myopic the process can be.

Sketchbooks come in many forms. For some, the book as an object is sacred. Having the book to hold, flip through and carry with them is vital, a portable chronicle. There are those who collect notebooks of all shapes and sizes, artists such as Chris Sullivan who says he's never bought paper, using laboratory notebooks, accounting ledgers, empty photo albums, heaps of dot-matrix paper—anything he finds. Others have bought the perfect book, the pages just the right off-white, the texture just so, and use only these, filling them and lining them up chronologically on their studio shelves. Some, such as Malcolm Sutherland, are incredibly prolific, drawing almost constantly, filling sketchbooks quickly (fig. 10). J J Villard filled 41 new, densely layered pages specifically for this project in less than a month (fig. 11). Many mentioned going back to their sketchbooks for ideas, using the books as a library

to be visited whenever they begin a new project. Then there are the pile keepers, artists who grab a bit of whatever is closest to them when lightning strikes. They accumulate stacks of drawings, all at arm's reach, as a project develops. Sometimes these heaps of creative sloughing get tossed when the film is completed, and sometimes the "best of" get pinned to the wall to curl and yellow.

It is a unique privilege to be allowed to glimpse inside these idiosyncratic visual journals, these dossiers of creative artifacts. You are a guest, a welcome spy. Enjoy these pages, get lost, crack the codes, be inspired, and start drawing.

10

8

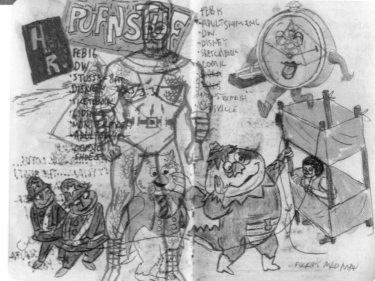

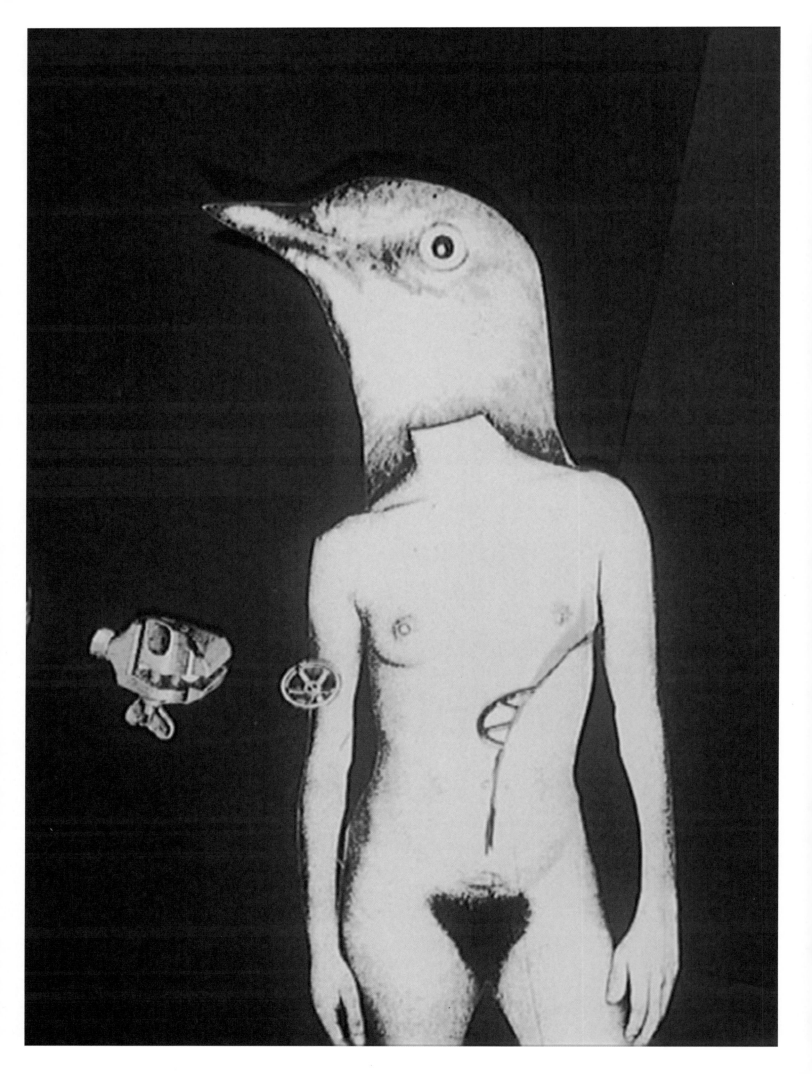

NANCY ANDREWS

"I make drawings on large paper as a way to externalize ideas, thoughts, and things that are more unformed and subconscious than thoughts. As Ima Plume says, near the end of The Haunted Camera (2006), *'There were things I could draw pictures of, and there were things that couldn't be drawn. More and more I was attracted to the second category. There were things I wanted to describe, but I didn't know how. There were things that I wanted to show but there was no way to show them.' For me, drawing is an attempt to get nearer to those things."*

Nancy Evelyn Andrews lives on the coast of Maine where she makes films, drawings, props, comic books, and objects. She works in hybrid forms combining storytelling, documentary, animation, puppetry, and research. Her characters and narratives are synthesized from various sources, including history, movies, popular educational materials, and autobiography. She has been the recipient of grants and fellowships, including the John Simon Guggenheim Memorial Foundation, LEF New England Moving Image Fund, Illinois Arts Council, the Franklin Furnace Fund for Performance Art (supported by the Jerome Foundation and New York State Council on the Arts), and National Endowment for the Arts. Her work has been presented by the Museum of Modern Art, New York; Pacific Film Archive; Ann Arbor Film Festival; Anthology Film Archives, New York; Jerusalem Film Festival; Flaherty Seminar, New York; Nova Cinema Bioscoop, Brussels; Film on the Rocks Yao Noi, Thailand; and Taiwan International Animation Festival, among others.

Six of her films are in the film collection of the Museum of Modern Art, New York, and one is in the School of the Art Institute of Chicago Film Collection. Her films include *Woods Marm* (1996), *Hedwig Page, Seaside Librarian* (1998), *The Reach of an Arm* (2000), *Monkeys and Lumps* (2003), *The Dreamless Sleep* (2004), *The Haunted Camera* (2006), *On a Phantom Limb* (2009), and *Behind the Eyes are the Ears* (2010). She studied at the School of the Art Institute of Chicago and received a MFA in 1995; her undergraduate studies were at the Maryland Institute, College of Art, where she received a BFA in 1983. Andrews is currently on the faculty at the College of the Atlantic, Maine, where she teaches video-making, animation, time-based arts, and film studies.

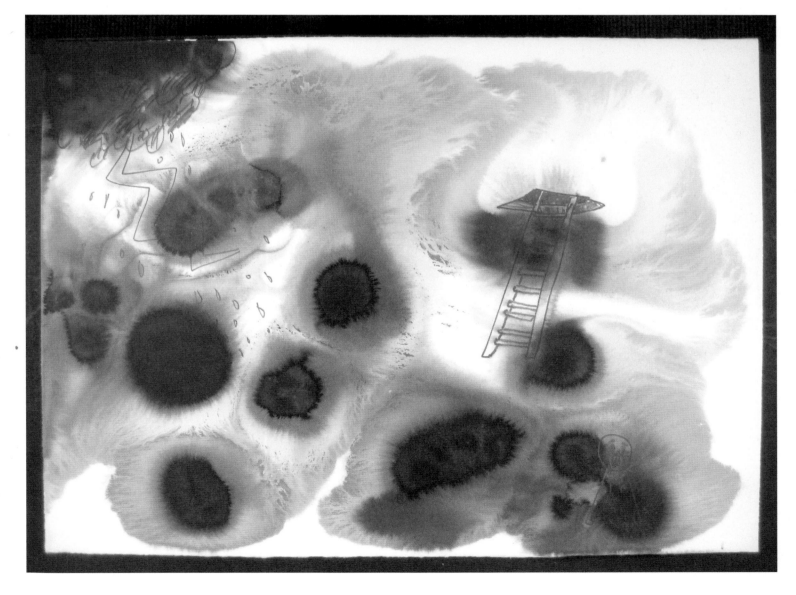

OPPOSITE Film still from *On a Phantom Limb*, 2009 ABOVE Drawing, ink on paper (22 x 30"), 2010

"After some major surgeries five years ago I was unable to perform the physically demanding tasks associated with animation for several months. But drawing was something I could do."

ABOVE Drawing for *On a Phantom Limb*, ink on paper with photocopy collage

OPPOSITE Drawings for *Behind the Eyes are the Ears*

PAGE 16 Drawings for *Behind the Eyes are the Ears*

PAGE 17, ABOVE Drawing for *Behind the Eyes are the Ears*, ink on paper with photocopy collage

BELOW Drawing for *On a Phantom Limb,* ink on paper with photocopy collage

PAGES 18–19 Drawing, ink on paper with photocopy collage

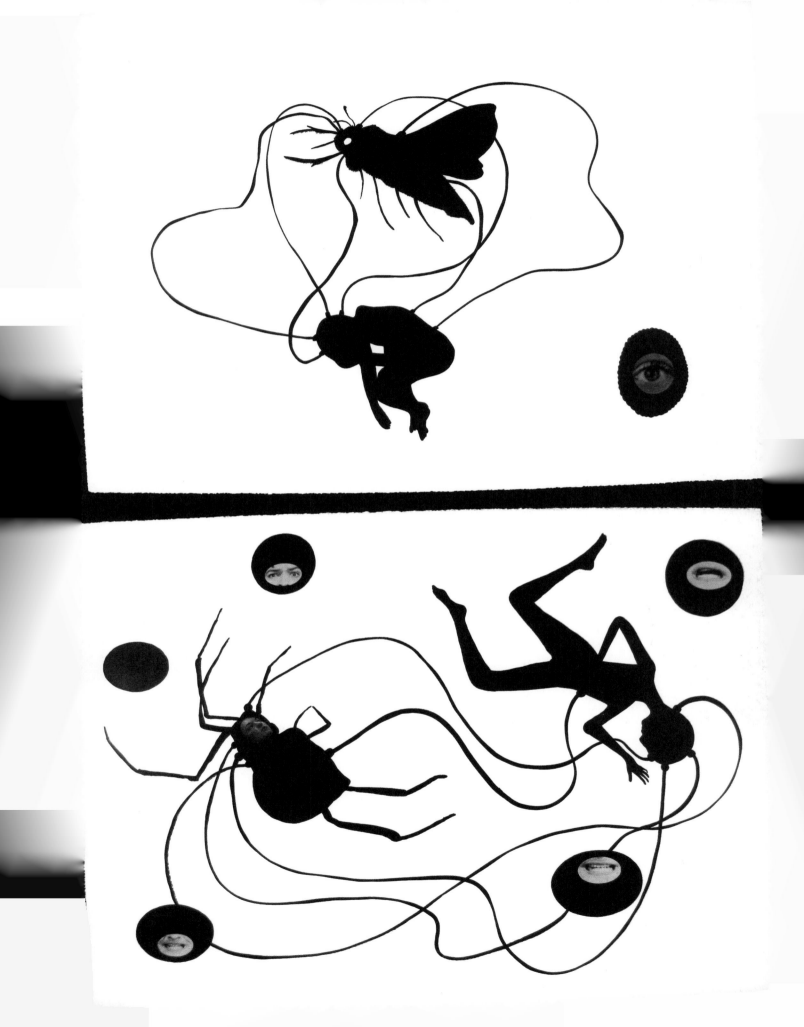

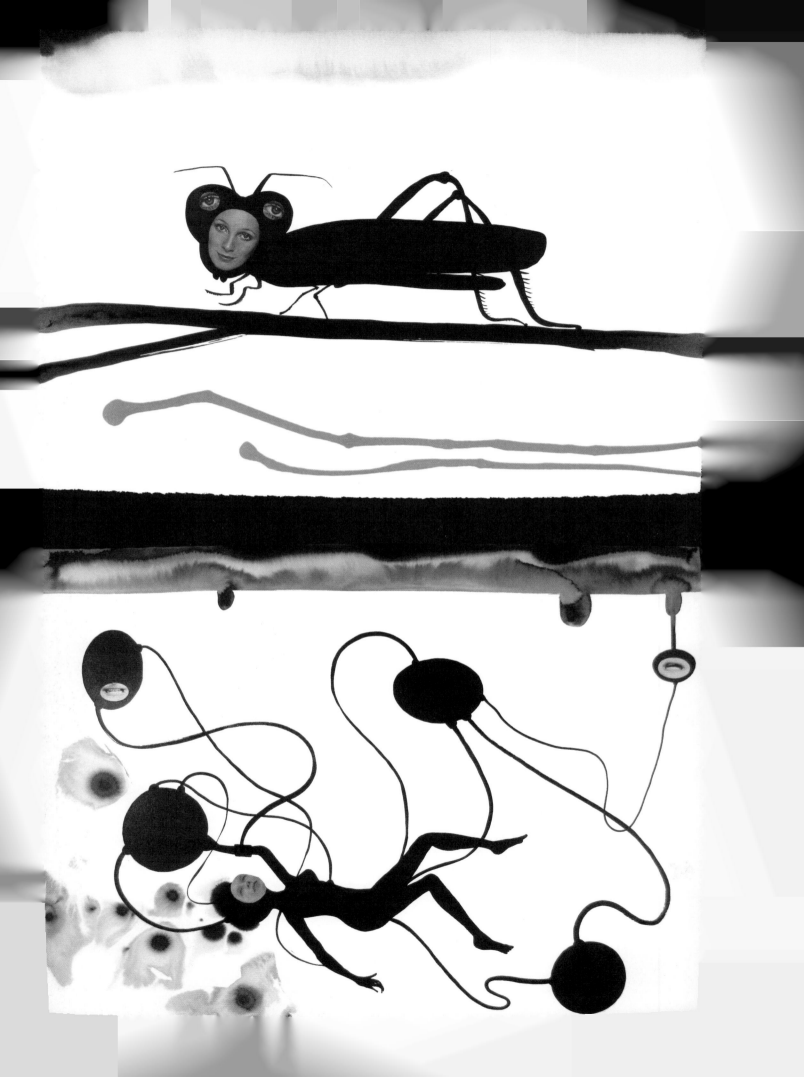

LILLI CARRÉ

"I like being able to capture the feeling of freely putting ink to paper and making drawings move without any restraint or set path, as well as using the medium to convey ideas while making the best of the possibilities of animation. My sketchbooks directly reflect my desire to work in these two ways, as they get stuffed with doodles of odds, ends, and faces drawn in the name of doodling, as well as the charts, lists, and narrative bits that I work to place within my films."

Lilli Carré was born in 1983 in Los Angeles, and currently lives and works in Chicago as an artist and illustrator. She primarily works in the forms of experimental animation, comics, and print. Her animated films have been shown at festivals throughout the US and abroad, including the Sundance Film Festival, and she is the co-founder of the Eyeworks Festival of Experimental Animation. Her books of comics are *Tales of Woodsman Pete* (2006), *The Lagoon* (2008), *Nine Ways to Disappear* (2009), and the recent collection *Heads or Tails* (2012). Her work has appeared in the *Believer* magazine, the *New Yorker*, the *New York Times*, *Best American Comics* and *Best American Nonrequired Reading*. Her recent films include *L'Ortolan* (2010), *Bleedin' Heart* (2011), *Disillusionment of Ten O'Clock* (2011), *The Jitters* (2011), and *Like a Lantern* (2012) which was made using many paper cut-outs and a Vandercook letterpress. She is currently filling her sketchbooks with thoughts and drawings for her next film and book projects.

"I do not treat my sketchbook like a personal or precious thing at all—it is like a big sloppy fishing net that scoops up all of my hare-brained ideas, many, many drawings of faces and foliage, plot outlines, notes on things to read about or look up later, and the occasional observational drawing from around the city."

"After sifting through the drawings and notes in my sketchbook, I usually start thumb-nailing out a more firm plot and/or sequence for a project. Sometimes, though, I get sick of planning things out and just like to start drawing my final animation without any plan at all and see where the drawings take me. I think this is one of the most wonderful feelings that can be achieved specifically through animation. Sure, it is one of the most insanely laborious mediums, making 12 drawings for every second that whizzes by, but what a reward it is to be able to draw freely and have these lines dance and immediately come to life!"

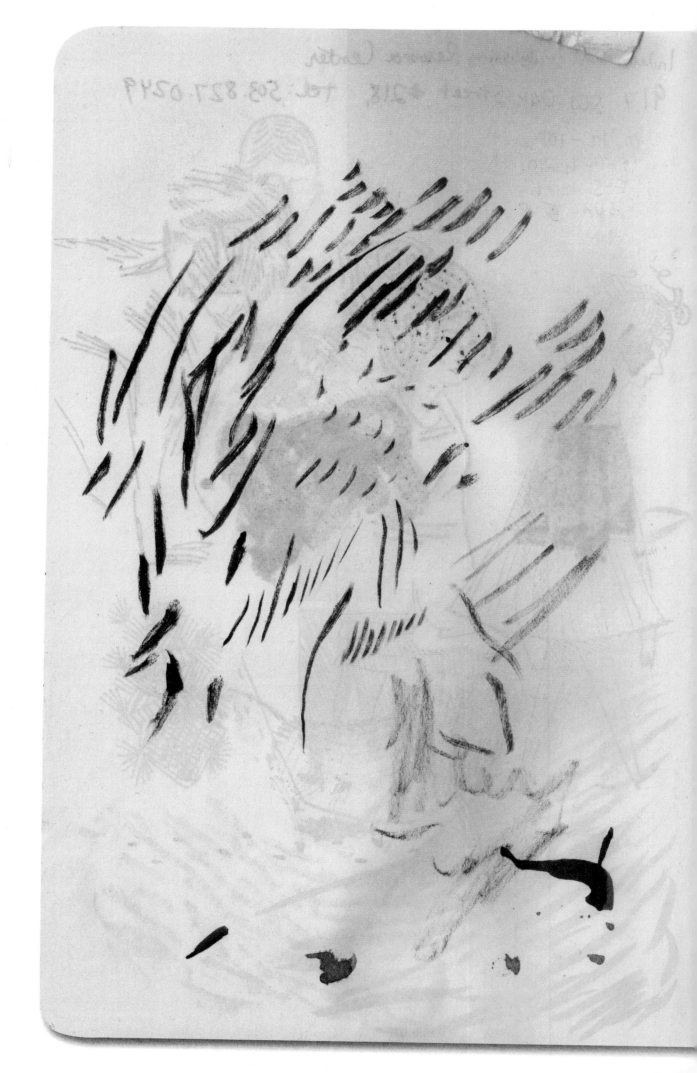

road twists
birds
oranges
sunset/night
women/romance
flowers

||postcards||

text – no text

karate illustrations
swimming illustrations

SOAPY!!

Limo/magazine sales/ellen + roger/popular girls/DOLL ROOM

Y2K - ~~1999~~ NEW YEARS MIDDLE OF NOWHERE - GREEN UNDEWEAR

DAD - GHANDI - NEIL YOUNG CARAMEL - TED BUNDY - GARAGE

BABYSITTERS
FIRES - EVACUATION - MR. COTT
DRUGS - FUNGUS - PRETEND - MY ROOM - TALL PERSON COSTUME PARTY

RAFT SLEEPING AT MOM'S RETREAT
WOMEN'S CAMP - MOM NAKED - SHAVED LEGS - GIRL FROM MHS
TRIP TO S.F. (LOS ALAMOS) - CAR - HORSE CHASING ANDREW
SEX ON TRAIL - RIDE HOME WITH WEIRD RANDY
"EXPLODED PEN" MASCARA LIE

SOAPY

Windy

hands it   light gleaming   her hand lifts   goes to take it   BURNS

balls through.   her head dissolves off

find car for burying.
Puritan portrait cracks like a puzzle.
foto of old sofa

go to Roosevelt Island Thrift Store = Books

Scene in Meth Lab: smoke rises to Make

Religious Clouds

tweakers melt candles iNTo Jackson Pollock

> Swat team in Colonial House.
1. out of chimney
2. windows
3. Break-in Door

MARTHA COLBURN

"Once I have a topic in mind, I begin collecting photographs, clippings from newspapers, poems, scraps off of the ground. I photocopy books from the library. I print out quotes and emails from friends. I collect color studies, historical painting references, literary notes, composers whose music I am listening to at the time and movies related to my subject. When I've collected all of this, sometimes over the course of two years, I get to a place where I have a deep, emotional relationship with the topic. At this point I would be able to make 100 different movies on my topic, or write a book, or a piece of music."

Martha Colburn was born in 1971 and raised in the Appalachian Mountains of Pennsylvania. She has completed over 40 films since 1994 which have been featured nationally and internationally in exhibitions and film festivals including: The Whitney Biennial (2006);

the Pompidou Centre, Paris; New Directors at Cannes Film Festival (2005); the Andy Warhol Museum, Pittsburgh; the Museum of Modern Art, New York; the Whitney Museum of American Art, New York; P.S.1 Contemporary Art Center, New York; the Serpentine Gallery, London; the Anthology Film Archive, New York; the Nanjing Art Institute Gallery, Nanjing, China; the Rotterdam International Film Festival; the Sundance Film Festival; and the New York Underground Film Festival. She contributed animation to Jeff Feuerzeig's documentary *The Devil and Daniel Johnston* (2006). Her most recent short films include *Myth Labs* (2008), *Join the Freedom Force* (music video for Knalpot, 2009), *'Literary Film' for Diana Wagman* (2009), *One and One Is Life* (2009), *Triumph of the Wild* (2009), and *DOLLS VS. DICTATORS* (2010). She has been based in Holland and New York since 2000.

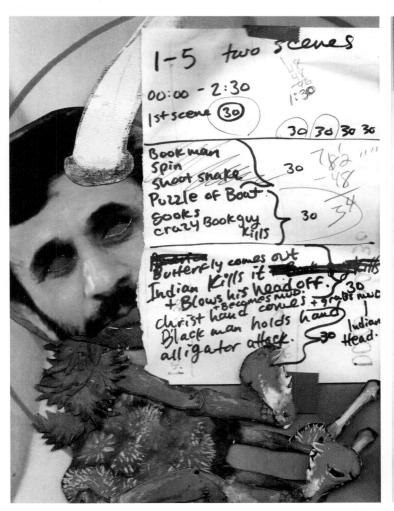

OPPOSITE *Myth Labs* script ABOVE *Triumph of the Wild* script

"I have strips of paper sometimes 20 feet long that plot the course of the film, like a script. I sketch on paper, which is then overlaid with photographs, painted over, and animated. The sketches become the materials in the film."

"Insanity is close to revelation."

ABOVE Film stills from *Triumph of the Wild*, 2009
OPPOSITE Puppets and painted parts for *Meet Me in Wichita*
PAGES 32–33 Multiplane set-up with cut-out puppets and painted backgrounds for *Myth Labs*

the pearce sisters

37.

LUIS COOK

"I have kept a sketchbook for over 25 years. They started conventionally but over time have evolved into scrapbooks. They are now filled with drawings, paintings, designs, photos, text, storyboards, telephone numbers, to-do lists and a long-standing collection of thumbprint self-portraits produced by hundreds of people I have either met or worked with. The books seem to grow organically, taking on a textural life of their own. They are a visual diary that provides me with a sense of continuity. To me, they are a creative lifeline and to an extent a security blanket. To others, they look like the insane visual ramblings of a serial killer. Or so I've been told."

Luis Cook was born in Berkshire, UK, in 1966. He has worked as a designer, illustrator, painter, photographer, teacher, art director, and director. In 1992 he returned to college to earn an MA in Animation at the Royal College of Art in London. After working for a few years at the BBC, he joined Aardman Animations in 1994. Since then he has directed many commercials, idents, promos, and short films. His short film *The Pearce Sisters* (2007) has won over 40 awards, including a BAFTA, the Cartoon d'Or, and the special jury prize at Annecy. Cook continues to direct, teach, draw, and paint and works in features development at Aardman. He is currently based in Bristol, UK.

OPPOSITE Sketchbook page, 2007 ABOVE Film stills from *The Pearce Sisters*, 2007
PAGES 36–41 Sketchbook pages, 2006

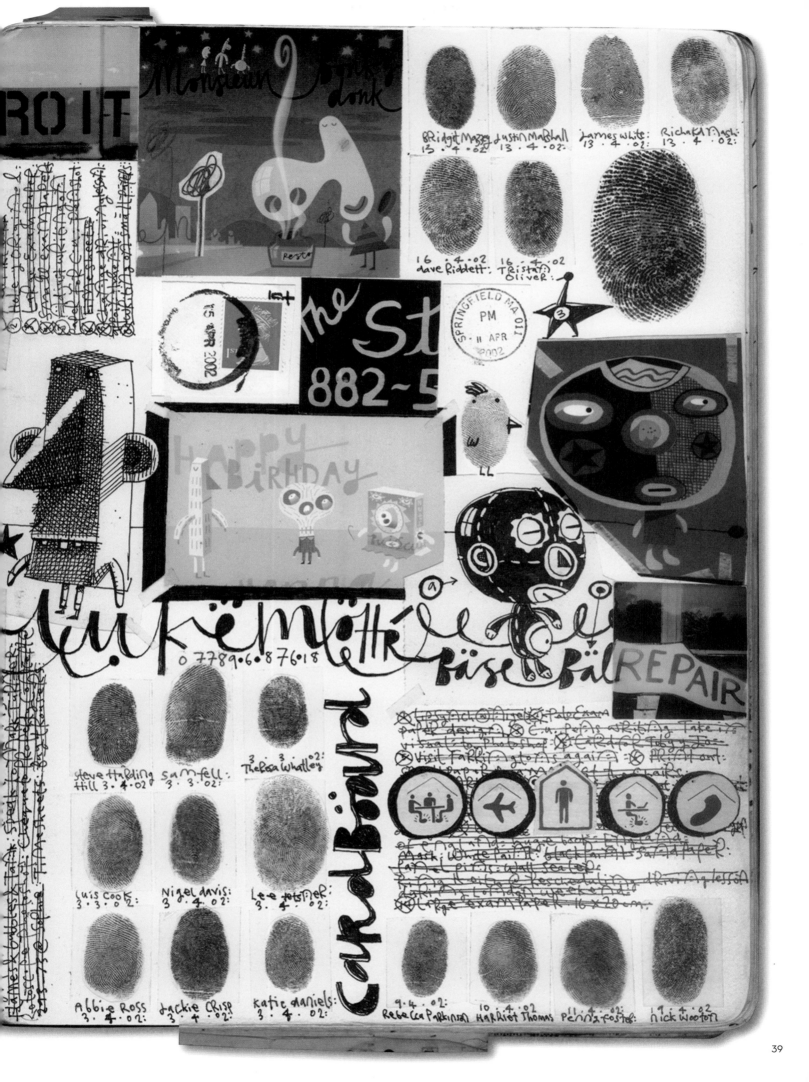

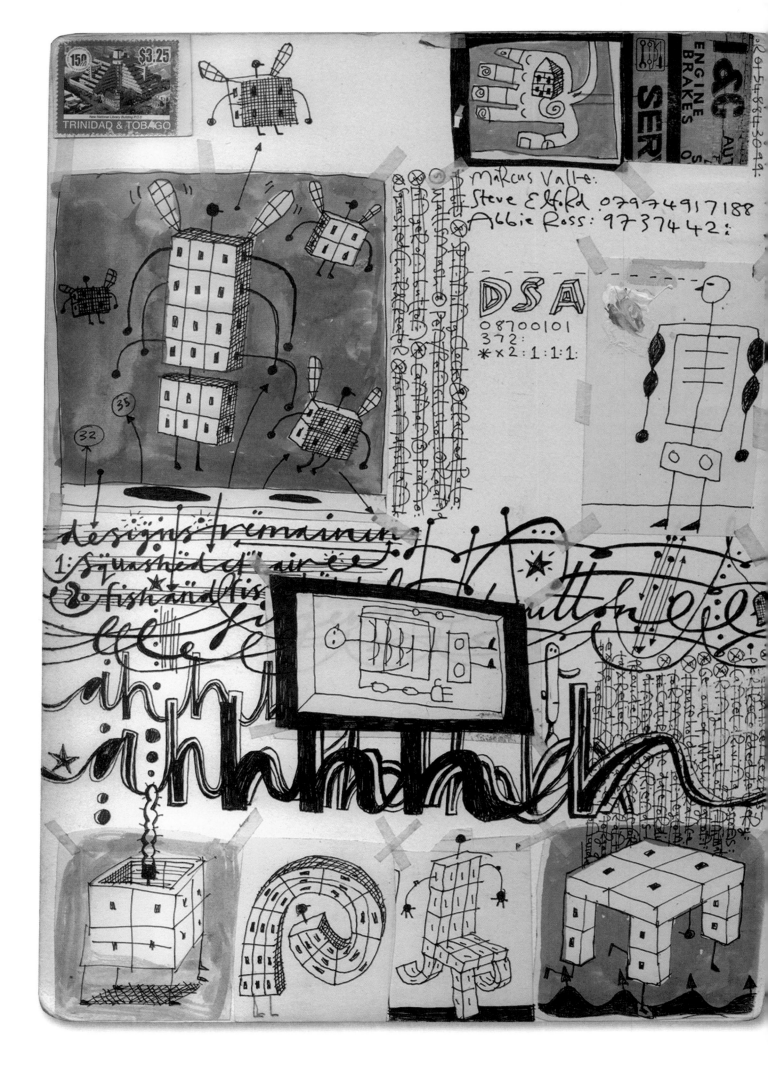

41

SUZANNE DEAKIN

"I 'collect' drawings and sketches in very small books: these are essentially the quickest images of people and situations that I can draw. It's a combination of feeling a little shy drawing in public, but also always wanting a minimal line to hold the most information. These are my collections of people, little crowds and groups in cafés, people on the street or passing by, people in the background really. I guess these are my 'holiday' drawings, but they continue to be the resource that I fall back on when needing a new face or character for a pitch or a brief. They're a very basic tool kit of spare body parts! It's also a bit like coming back to the beginning, the reason I started in animation—I'm a people watcher, I like the way people move, stand, express themselves, and my sketchbooks are now a collection."

Suzanne Deakin studied Film and Animation at the University of Wales, Newport, followed by further studies in Animation at the Royal College of Art, London. While living in London, she worked at the Museum of the Moving Image, and began to make her way into the commercial sector, working as an animator in a number of production companies. In 2000, she joined the newly formed Slinky Pictures as a Director, and was commissioned to work on various commercial, TV, and web projects over the next 10 years. She has directed advertisements for Nokia, Channel 4, BBC1, the Cancer Treatment Centers of America, TalkBack Productions for BBC, and Live Earth. Deakin directed a 2D animation spot, *Olay Lines* (2007), which won a Silver at the London International Advertising Awards. Some of her early films include *Dry Shave* (1995), *Pocket* (1997), and *Ladies and Gentlemen* (1998). She currently lives and works in London.

ABOVE *"Diagram—this is the kind of working-out storyboard I'd do to figure out the direction of movement throughout something, so no actual reference to characters really, just motion happening on the screen and how it cuts together. This was for a short film for a Portuguese children's channel."*

OPPOSITE AND PAGE 44 *"Ibiza people collection—sketches I do when I go places. These are quite 'holiday' in some ways, but I also use them to collect 'types' of people which I can then use as reference for other projects."*

"'The sketchbook,' as an idea and as something useful, has completely changed for me through the development of my career."

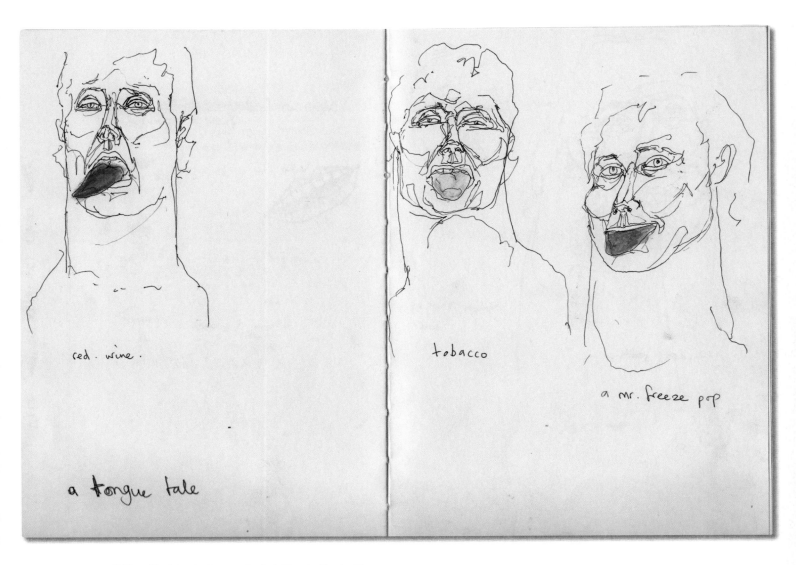

red. wine.

tobacco

a mr. freeze pop

a tongue tale

"When I look back at my early sketchbooks they're like these precious objects, everything was worked, the covers, the pages bulging, paint cracking, stuff glued in. There were lots of ideas, most of them crappy and immature, yet some were the simple nuggets of the small film they could become. In fact, the drawings or sketches that did turn into films were often the smallest and simplest, rather than the pages that were most overworked and illustrated."

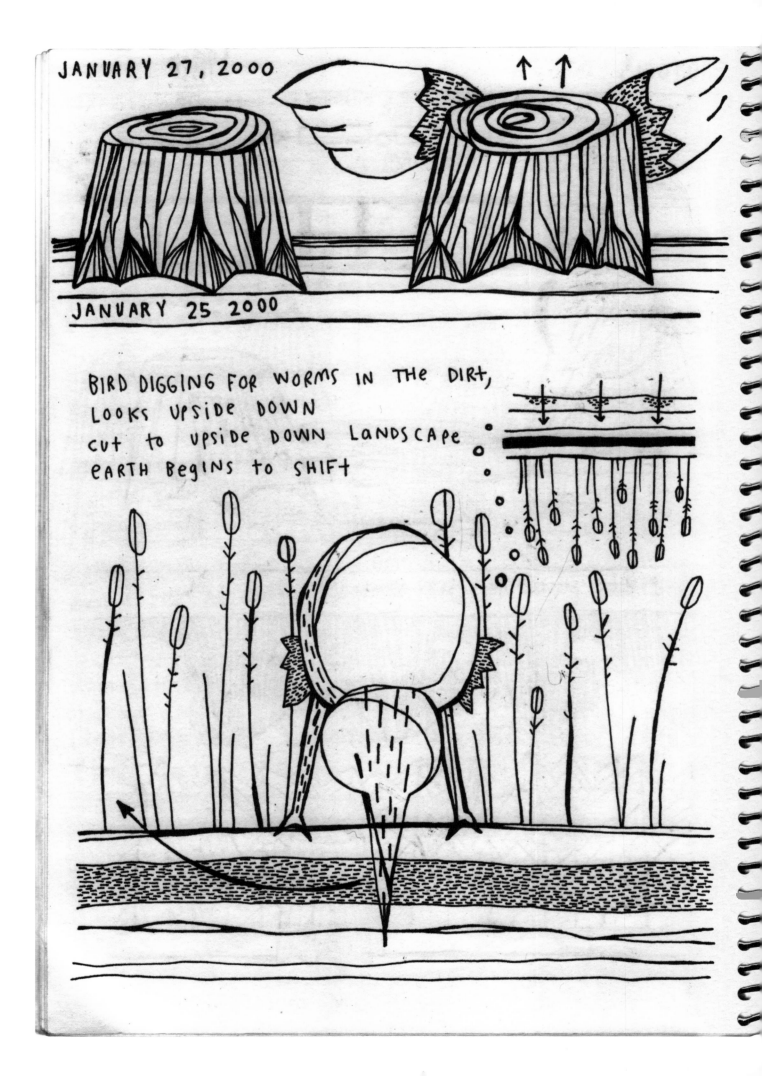

JO DERY

"My process begins with accumulation, by maintaining a drawing practice that generates both images and text. Compelling material is spun into the fabric of a narrative, often interwoven with inquiries into various fields of knowledge: science, philosophy, and economics, to name a few."

Jo Dery is an artist who experiments with storytelling. Her works include short films/videos, drawings, prints, illustration, installation, and artist/small-press book publications. Her animations have screened at festivals nationally and internationally, including the Ann Arbor Film Festival and the Rotterdam International Film Festival. She has been awarded grants for her film/video work from the LEF Foundation, the Rhode Island State Council on the Arts, and The Free History Project. She has exhibited her drawings and prints in Providence, New York, San Francisco, Portland, and Los Angeles. Dery has completed residencies at the MacDowell Colony and the Virginia Center for the Creative Arts, as well as participating in an animation workshop at the Academy of Fine Arts in Krakow, Poland. Most recently, she designed an installation project for the DeCordova Museum Biennial at the DeCordova Sculpture Park and Museum in Massachusetts. Her films include *The Last, the Rest* (2000), *Echoes of Bats and Men* (2005), *Woodpecker in Snowshoes* (2008), and *Peeks* (2009). She was awarded a BFA in Film/Animation/Video from the Rhode Island School of Design and an MFA in Interdisciplinary Arts from Goddard College, Plainfield, Vermont. In 2011, she relocated from Providence, Rhode Island, to Chicago, where she is currently an Assistant Professor of Animation at DePaul University's School of Cinema and Interactive Media.

OPPOSITE Sketchbook drawings for *The Last, the Rest* ABOVE Film still from *The Last, the Rest*, 2000

47

"Drawing and writing in a stream-of-consciousness fashion are the most direct means by which I have created a dialogue with my intuitive creative processes."

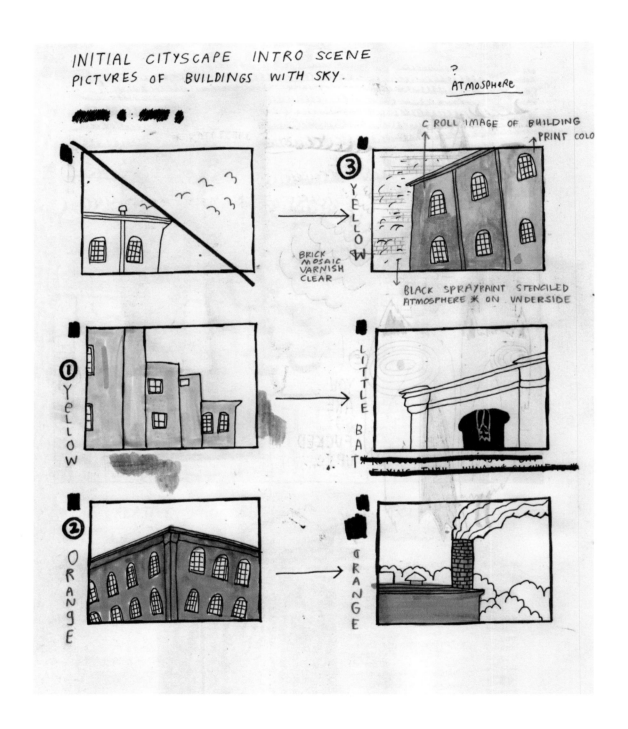

ABOVE Storyboard for *Echoes of Bats and Men*
OPPOSITE, ABOVE Concept art for *Echoes of Bats and Men*
OPPOSITE, BELOW Film stills from *Echoes of Bats and Men*, 2005
PAGES 50–51 Sketchbook drawing

"I reference my sketchbooks when I begin drawing a comic or making a film, or when I am asked to draw an illustration. The nonsensical language that is scribbled among my drawings plays an important role in creating the stories found in my books and films."

listening
tube

tubes

PAUL DRIESSEN

"I have the luxury of making the films I enjoy making. Although they might look similar in style, each film is based on a different idea, something new that I like to explore in animation. Whereas my early films were often limited in the way I used animation, the older I get the more I elaborate on the animation itself. I'm still fascinated by how hand-drawn animation can surprise you when you see it on the big screen. Scribbling down ideas goes much faster than drawing them. I have a map sitting amongst my files which is called IDEAS. It's my kind of sketchbook."

Paul Driessen was born in Nijmegen, the Netherlands, in 1940 and drew cartoons from an early age. After graduating from the Utrecht School of the Arts in 1964,

Driessen worked in animation at a commercial TV and film studio near Amsterdam. In 1967 George Dunning invited him to London to work on the Beatles film *Yellow Submarine* (1968). Dunning, a Canadian, inspired Driessen to emigrate to Canada and from 1970 he produced most of his personal films at the National Film Board of Canada. Since 1976 he has also animated and directed many of his films for independent producers in the Netherlands. His filmography includes *Elbowing* (1980), *The End of the World in Four Seasons* (1995), the Oscar-nominated *3 Misses* (1999), *The Boy Who Saw the Iceberg* (2000), *2D or Not 2D* (2004), and *Oedipus* (2011). Driessen has also taught animation at the University of Kassel in Germany. Under his guidance his students have won two Oscars. He lives in Montreal, Canada.

OPPOSITE AND ABOVE Storyboards for *2D or Not 2D*

PAGES 54–55 Storyboard set-up for the split-screen film *The Boy Who Saw the Iceberg*, 2000; on page 54, the "color" panels of the boy's "real" life and on page 55, the "monochrome" panels of his fantasy life

"When I was young, I spent a lot of time by myself and I used most of that time to draw cartoons."

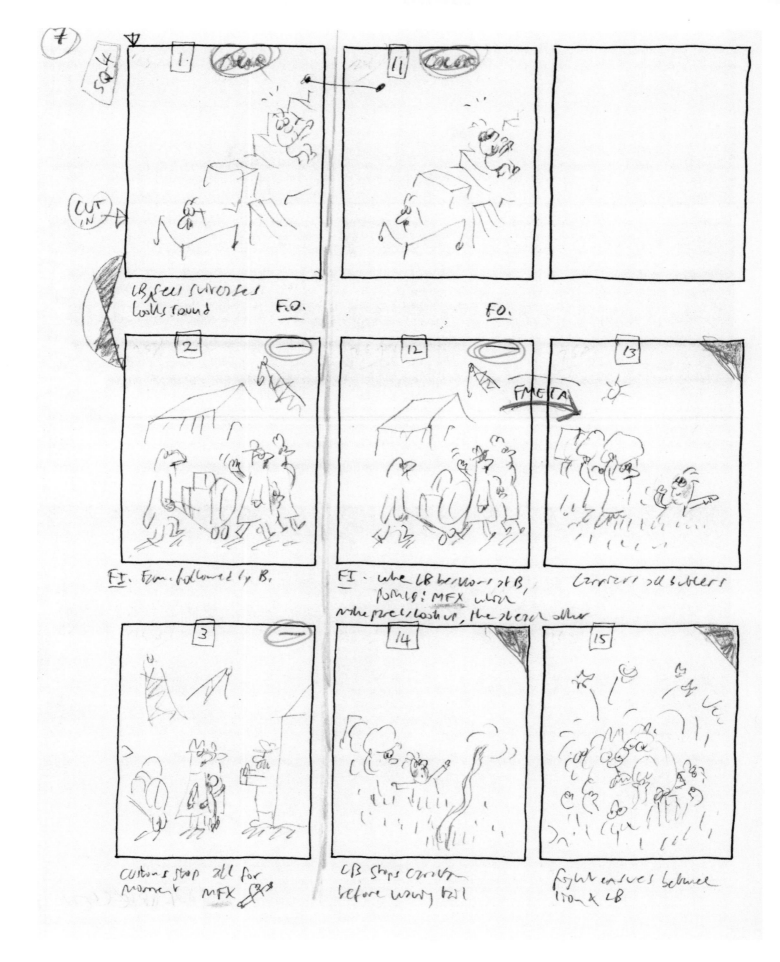

55

FÉLIX DUFOUR-LAPERRIÈRE

"For me, the sketchbooks make it possible to keep traces of thoughts and ideas, to think effectively on a trip or on vacation, to work a little while travelling, to build an ensemble of concepts, ideas, images, and vocabulary that are needed to enrich a project. It enables me to make my ideas clearer."

Félix Dufour-Laperrière was born in 1981 in Chicoutimi, Quebec. He studied, lives, and works in Montreal. His films have been presented and awarded in numerous national and international galleries, museums, and festivals. His films include *Black Ink on Sky Blue* (2003), *Head* (2006) with Dominic Etienne Simard, *One, Two, Three, Dusk* (2006), *Variations sur Marilou* (2007), *Rosa Rosa* (2008), *M* (2009), *Strips* (2010), and *Half Light Dynamics* (2012). He is currently developing his first feature.

ABOVE Drawing after *The Sinking of the Lusitania* by Winsor McCay OPPOSITE Visual tests for *Rosa Rosa*

Comp 1 (0.00.18.07).psd   RGB

FD

Rosa Rosa

Comp 1 (0.00.04.20).psd   RGB

Crayon 3B — gesso medium mat — gesso - impression

"My creative process is a constant reflection: observing the surroundings, thinking about contemporary political, social, or artistic issues. I write a lot, draw a little, but most often I start making images with a certain technique. After that, I try to combine the various possibilities of this technique and give a direction, an orientation within the resulting images and short animated sequences."

ABOVE AND OPPOSITE Preliminary images/tests for an upcoming abstract short film; ink on paper and blown ink over stencil (above) and stickers (opposite)

PAGES 60–61 Film stills from *Rosa Rosa*, 2008

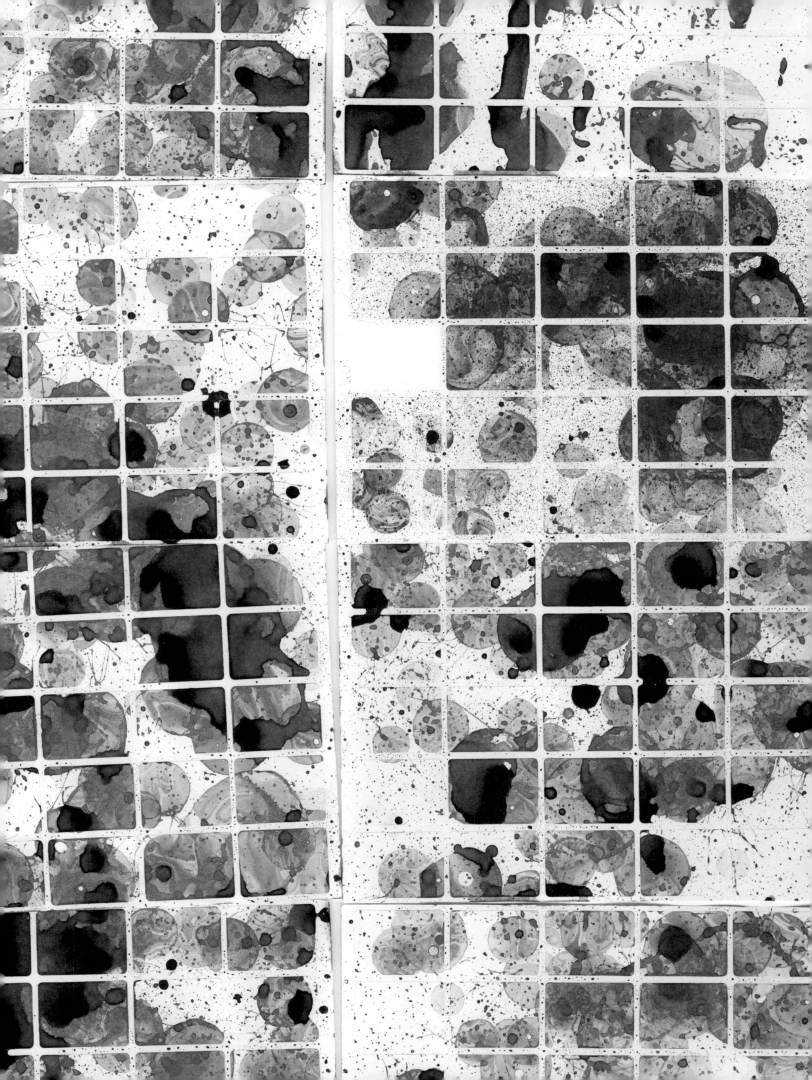

ADAM ELLIOT

"My journal and my drawings are extremely personal to me and are where all my ideas, thoughts, beliefs, emotions, and inevitable stories are born. If I were to ever lose them, I'm unsure what I'd do or what I'd become. It would be like losing my hands or my sight."

Adam Elliot was born in 1972 and grew up on a shrimp farm in the Australian outback with his father, Noel, a retired acrobatic clown, his mother Valerie, a hairdresser, and three siblings. In 1996 he completed a post-graduate diploma at the Victorian College of the Arts, Melbourne, specializing in animation. This is where he made his first film *Uncle*. He has made five films that have collectively received over 100 awards, including an Oscar for *Harvie Krumpet* (2003) and the Annecy Cristal for *Mary and Max* (2009).

OPPOSITE Film stills from *Mary and Max*, 2009
ABOVE Character sketches for *Mary and Max*: Vera Dinkle (left) and Reoccurring old lady (right)
PAGE 64 Character sketches for *Mary and Max*: Max (above, left), Len (middle), and Mr. Biscuit (below)
PAGE 65 Character sketches for *Mary and Max*: Kevin the Pug (above, left), Grandpoppy Ralph (above, right), and Ivy (below)

"I call my journal and drawings my 'triggers.' Some may never end up in my Clayographies but each could be that first domino to cause the creative juices to go from a trickle to a torrent."

"My drawings are the ingredients for an enormous and expensive cake I serve up to my audience as an animated film. It is a very complex and slow cake to bake and so the ingredients have to be the best, the tastiest, and most original."

JANIE GEISER

"The Red Book *sprang from several sources. The first was a dream that I had, which involved several images that became key to the film. In the dream I was watching, as in a cropped close-up, the lower arms and hands of several people scratching hieroglyphs into the dirt. These changed into architects' hands, using rulers and T-squares to create their plans. An outline of a house began to emerge... Later in the dream I uncovered a face under the dirt; later I uncovered a book. The house appeared in the distance, balanced on the top of a mountain. I began to draw these images, and then to paint them in a book that I made especially for these images. At that time I was in the habit of making small, painted books, usually as diaries of daily events, which sometimes included dreams.*"

Janie Geiser was born in Baton Rouge, Louisiana, and is an experimental filmmaker and visual/theater artist. Her films have been screened at the Whitney Museum of American Art, New York; the Solomon R. Guggenheim Museum, New York; the Museum of Modern Art, New York; Pacific Film Archives, Berkeley; the Wexner Center for the Arts, Columbus, Ohio; the San Francisco Cinematheque; Los Angeles Filmforum; and at numerous festivals, including seven New York film festivals, and international film festivals in Toronto, San Francisco, Hong Kong, London, and Rotterdam. Her film *The Red Book* (1994) was selected for the National Film Registry of the Library of Congress, and her film *The Fourth Watch* (2000) was selected by *Film Comment* magazine as one of the top ten experimental films of the 2000s. Geiser's recent films include *Ghost Algebra* (2009), *The Floor of the World* (2010), *Kindless Villain* (2010), and *Ricky* (2011). She is on the faculty of the School of Theater at CalArts, Valencia, California, and is the Co-Artistic Director of Automata—a non-profit dedicated to object performance, puppetry, experimental film, and other lost or neglected art forms. Geiser is based in Los Angeles.

OPPOSITE The first page from the first of three hand-painted red books by Janie Geiser that inspired the film *The Red Book* ABOVE Sketchbook page, dream images

"These issues of memory and identity were still quite compelling to me, and they began to merge with the imagery of the red books that I had been making. I started creating cut-outs and backgrounds, and accumulating collage materials to explore these images and ideas in an animated film. While the film's narrative is elliptical and not entirely explicit, in my internal narrative the woman in the film loses her memory after a fall—whether it is suicide or accident is left ambiguous."

"The Red Book was my first fully animated film, so I was quite excited by the possibilities of the form. I had made several short films involving puppets and cut-outs, but had filmed them live with puppeteers moving the objects. Working on The Red Book, I was exhilarated by the freedom that was offered by the form—anything could move anywhere, gravity could be ignored, scale could shift, images in the same frame could move at different rates. These formal possibilities opened up the film frame to me in a new way."

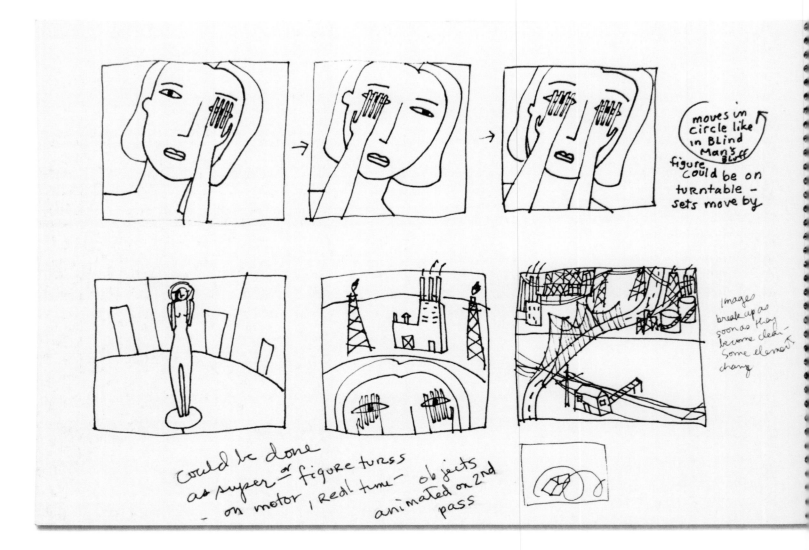

ABOVE Storyboard for *The Red Book*

OPPOSITE Film stills from the animated film *The Red Book*, 1994

PAGES 70-71 Pages from the painted book *The Red Book*

PHILIPPE GRAMMATICOPOULOS

"I'm interested in working with universal themes. Therefore, I integrate these ideas more generally into a reflection on the concerns of our modern world, for example, the exclusion and fear of the foreigner in **The Process,** *GMO in* **The Bellies** *and bioethics and human reproductive cloning in* **The Regulator.***"*

Philippe Grammaticopoulos was born in Brussels, Belgium, in 1970. He graduated from the Saint-Luc Institute of Brussels, majoring in comic strip illustration, and went on to gain a degree in digital animation at Supinfocom (Ecole Supérieure d'Informatique de Communication) in Valenciennes, France. His films, *The Process* (2000), *The Regulator* (2004), and *The Bellies* (*Les Ventres*, 2009), have received multiple awards in festivals internationally. He was presented with a Golden Lion at the Cannes Film Festival for his film *Signature* (commissioned by Amnesty International, 2007). His other works include comic strips, children's books, and illustrations for newspapers such as *Le Monde*. Grammaticopoulos currently lives and works in Paris.

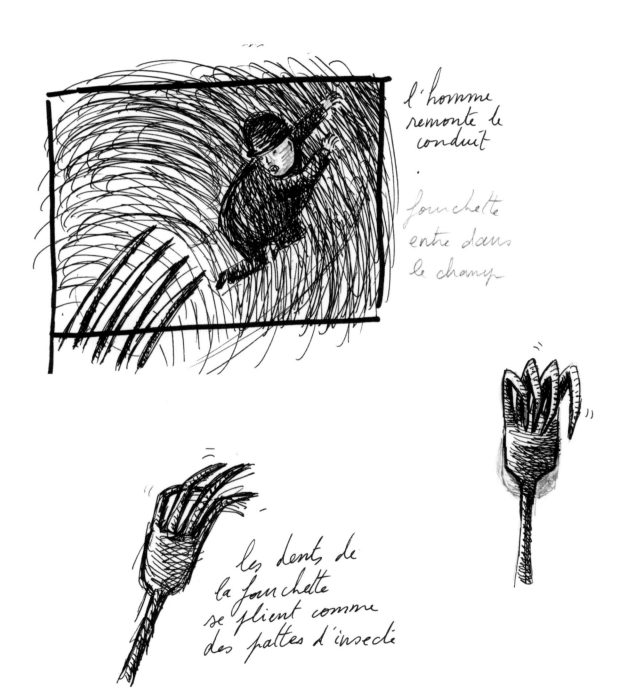

l'homme remonte le conduit

fourchette entre dans le champ

les dents de la fourchette se plient comme des pattes d'insecte

ABOVE *The Bellies (Les Ventres)* notes and ideas OPPOSITE Storyboard frames for *The Bellies (Les Ventres)*, 2009

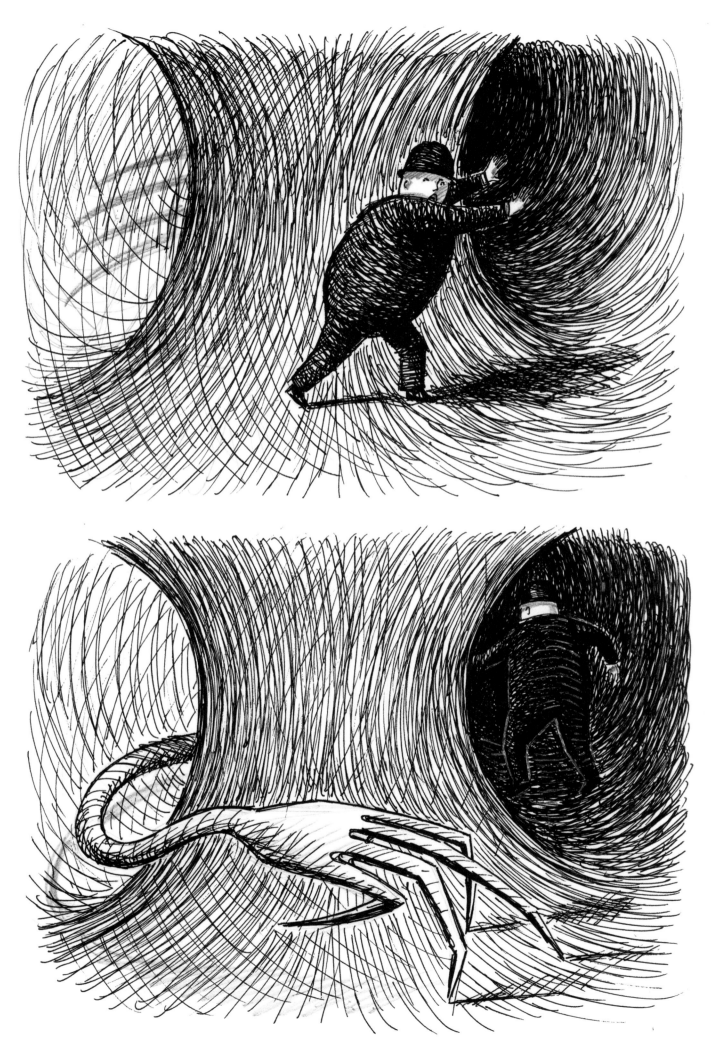

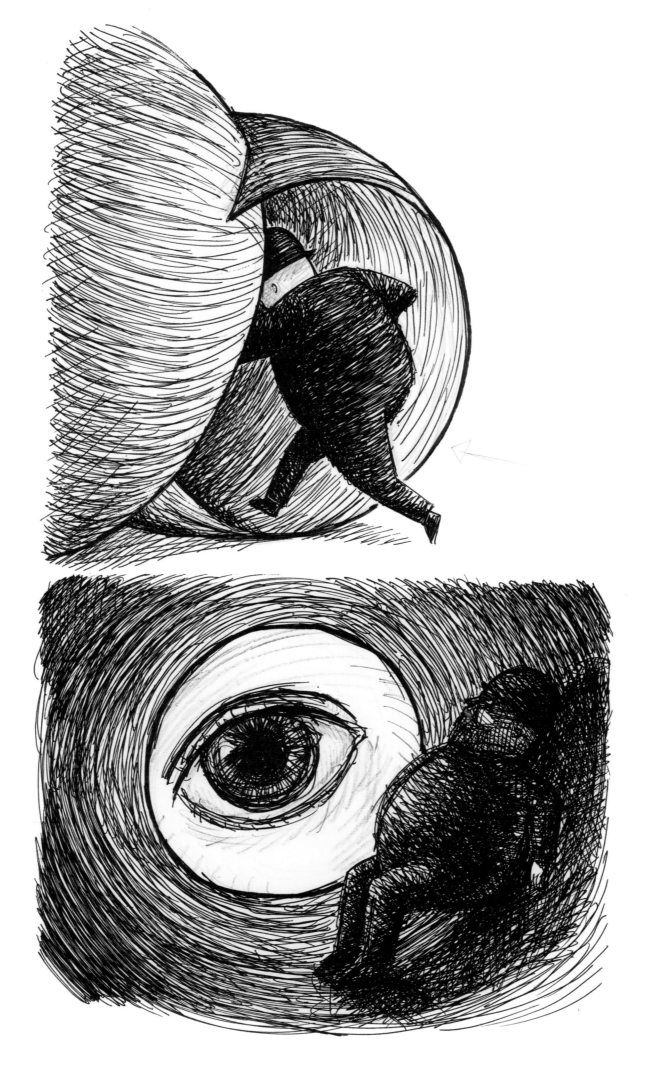

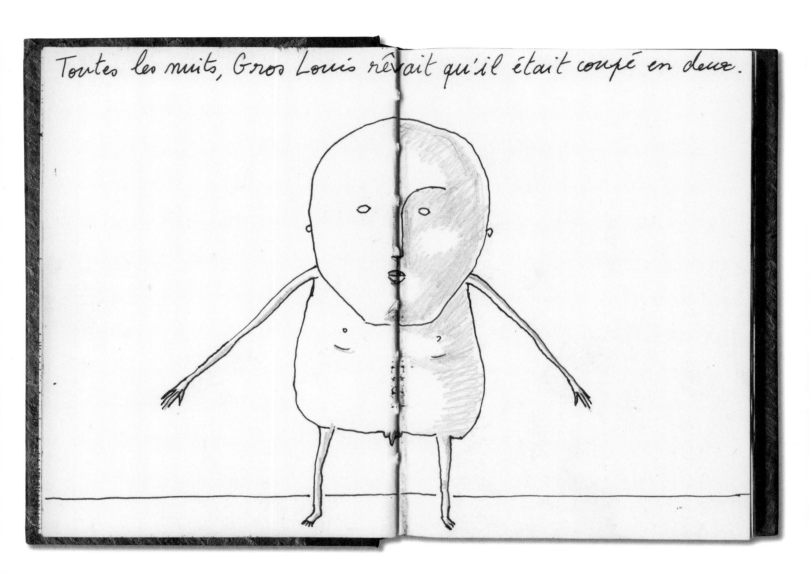

Toutes les nuits, Gros Louis rêvait qu'il était coupé en deux.

PIERRE-LUC GRANJON

"Sometimes I don't use my sketchbook at all, but it is important for me to know that if I need it, I have it. And, as I feel guilty if I don't draw, I end up drawing."

Pierre-Luc Granjon was born in France in 1973. He spent one year at the University of Geneva studying history of art and then went on to study at the School of Applied Arts, Lyon. In 1998 he became a model maker at Folimage and then started animating for the television series *Hilltop Hospital*. During this time he made his first two films: *A Little Adventure* (*Une Petite escapade*, 2001) and *The Other Kids' Castle* (*Le Château des autres*, 2003).

He then made *The Child with No Mouth* (*L'enfant sans bouche*, 2004), produced by Corridor Studios, and *The White Wolf* (*Le Loup blanc*, 2006), produced by Sacrebleu Productions, which was awarded at festivals worldwide. Granjon has also directed four 26-minute puppet films: *Léon in Wintertime* (*L'Hiver de Léon*, co-directed with Pascal Le Nôtre, 2007), *Molly in Springtime* (*Le Printemps de Mélie*, 2009), and co-directed with Antoine Lanciaux: *Bonifacio in Summertime* (*L'été de Boniface*, 2011) and *Poppety in the Fall* (*L'Automne de Pougne*, 2012). He is currently working on a new film called *The Big Beast* (*La Grosse bête*) produced by Les Décadrés.

OPPOSITE AND ABOVE Sketchbook drawings for *The Army of Rabbits* (*L'Armée des lapins*), a long-term feature project

"For all of my short films, I never start by writing. I have a picture in my head, which I try to draw, and then I build a story around that image. For instance, The White Wolf (Le Loup blanc) was born from an image in my mind. A family is sitting around a table while the mother is getting ready to kill a rabbit that the father has just brought home. The two children are watching this scene without flinching, no doubt because they are used to it. Around this image, I created a short tale that verged on the nightmarish."

ABOVE Drawing for *The Army of Rabbits (L'Armée des lapins)*
OPPOSITE Early sketches for *The Big Beast (La Grosse bête)*
PAGES 80–81 Sketchbook drawing

BRENT GREEN

"*When I first started making films, I was obsessive. I storyboarded every single second. Every dancing scene I would map out. I used to do it so I wouldn't go off track. Now, I don't. I do map out the mouth movements. I map out, sometimes, the basic scene, but it's more just having an idea of what I want to get across, but I control it a lot less. I've actually loved the human error of it, from the beginning...which you can tell. I'm running no shortage of human error! I think that's something that Kentridge got right away. It's more honest. It's a lot less controlled. It's a little more risky.*"[1]

Brent Green, born in 1978, works in the Appalachian hills of rural Pennsylvania and is a self-taught visual artist, filmmaker, and storyteller. His films have screened, often accompanied by live music, in film and art settings, in venues such as the Museum of Modern Art, New York; the J. Paul Getty Museum, Los Angeles; the Walker Art Center, Minneapolis; the Hammer Museum, Los Angeles; the Rotterdam International Film Festival; the Sundance Film Festival; even extending to rooftops, warehouses, and galleries around the world. His sculptural work and large-scale installations are often displayed alongside his animated films, most recently in solo exhibitions at the ASU Art Museum, Arizona; SITE Santa Fe; Art Without Walls, New York; DiverseWorks Houston; and the Berkeley Art Museum. Green has crafted his rickety folk, punk style into everything from a hacked LCD and steel animation machine (*To Many Men Strange Fates Are Given*, 2012) to a feature-length pixelated film (*Gravity Was Everywhere Back Then*, 2010) to his many hand-drawn and stop-motion shorts, including *Hadacol Christmas* (2005), *Paulina Hollers* (2006), *Carlin* (2007), and *Weird Carolers* (2008). Green's next project, *Anatomical Maps with Battle Plans*, is a feature-length film that weaves together his fabled family history, film collage, and his precise voice as he continues to develop his uniquely hand-crafted visions.

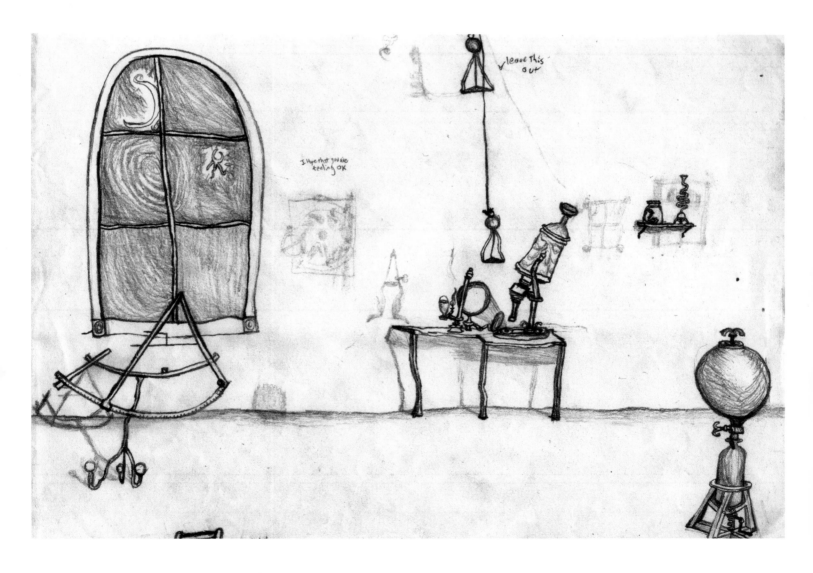

OPPOSITE Storyboard for untitled Vic Chesnutt Project, 2004 ABOVE Background sketch for *Hadacol Christmas*, 2005
1 Brooks, Blair Asbury. "Brent Green: On Kentridge, Animation, and Making the Worst Circus Ever." Trent Fine Art Advisory, May 31, 2010

"I was always writing stories and songs and I just wasn't getting across the whole idea…like it wasn't quite good enough really. So I decided that if I could do an animated film, I could control everything. I could control each picture, the focal point, the music, the lighting, like every single thing I could control and so I could get across what I was lacking in storytelling or in understanding how people respond to the story. So this was a way of skipping that and figuring it out later." [2]

We make these things more complicated than they need to be.

ABOVE Sketch for untitled animation, 2005
OPPOSITE Film stills from *Paulina Hollers*, 2006
2 Interview with filmmaker Brent Green, Houston Movies, www.29–95.com, Ramon Medina Movies, 12.14 pm on November 5, 2010

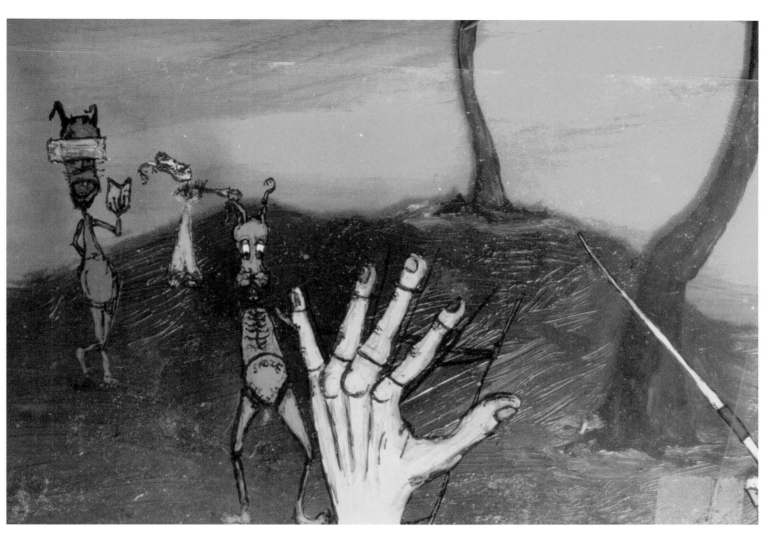

1.

2.

TV FLICKER

COACH HOUSE

LAURA HEIT

"I think of my sketchbook as a safe place to try things out—to play with ideas. I find myself making maps of ideas, taping in stamps and images from newspapers, scraps of inspiration, quick thumbnails of storyboards—or sequences, and lists, lots of lists."

Laura Heit employs stop-motion, live-action puppetry, hand drawing, and computer animation in her short films. Her work has screened at museums and film festivals around the world, including the Walker Art Center, Minneapolis; Museum of Modern Art, New York; Solomon R. Guggenheim Museum, New York; Anthology Film Archives, New York; Millennium Film Workshop, New York; Annecy, Rotterdam, Taiwan, Ann Arbor, and London International Film Festivals, as well as the Black Maria Film + Video Festival, New Jersey and Public Broadcasting Service, and others. She also works in puppetry,

experimental theater, and live performance. Her acclaimed miniature puppet show, *The Matchbox Shows*, in which Heit plays ringmaster to a tiny cabaret, has been touring for over ten years at St. Ann's Warehouse, Brooklyn, REDCAT, Los Angeles, and Walt Disney Concert Hall, Los Angeles. She has been the recipient of awards and grants from MacDowell Colony (2007 and 2009), Channel Four Television, London; the British Film Council; the Durfee Foundation, Los Angeles; ARC grant; Jim Henson Foundation; Puppeteers of America; and MTV. She has a BFA in Film from the School of the Art Institute of Chicago, and an MFA from the Royal College of Art, London. From 2007 until 2011 she was co-director of the Experimental Animation program at CalArts in Valencia, California. Born in Minneapolis, she lives and works in Portland, Oregon.

OPPOSITE Sketch for the film *Look for Me* ABOVE Film stills from *Look for Me*, 2005

*"I almost never draw anything here (in my sketchbook) that feels finished—
it's like a book of starting places."*

"I always have a few books going, one for rough sketches, one for lists, and one for daily diary drawings. I like the object of the notebook, the paper—the binding. I have a collection of blank books I've picked up all over the world waiting to be filled. It's far more satisfying to draw in a book than on the computer or even scrap paper. I find the book a place I can archive my thoughts, for me it's a logbook of my visual ideas. I can open the book and come back to where I was a few days ago—or even a month ago. In that sense it's more of a space or place I can enter and exit just by opening and closing its pages. I find the blank pages comforting, it's an uncritical place to play, to mess around. Drawing is private in its action, there is no pretence of performance or permanence—it's free from critique."

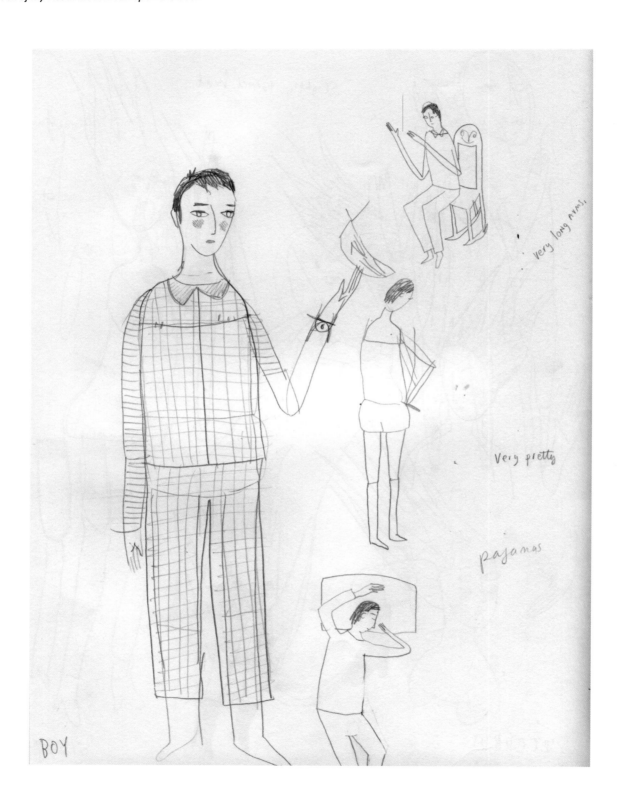

ABOVE AND OPPOSITE Puppet designs for a performance/film

PAGES 92-93 Sketchbook drawing for a ghost story

Haxau

slightly turned head

long arms
to hold you)

SUCCUBUS

IMA
NO SEM

BASTAR GIRLS in

ISABEL HERGUERA

"I take my sketchbook everywhere with me, sometimes having it with me gives me comfort. As soon as I open those pages I feel at home. Sometimes I draw when I am feeling at peace, but mainly I draw when I am looking for it. The act of drawing is private, but once the drawing is done it doesn't feel mine anymore. It becomes detached from me. It becomes public."

Isabel Herguera discovered animation thanks to a friend who showed her how to work a Bolex camera and gave her his animation equipment. After graduating in Experimental Animation from CalArts in Valencia, California, she worked in many different animation studios in Los Angeles. In 2003, she returned to Donosita, Spain, and from 2003 to 2011 she directed ANIMAC, the International Animation Film Festival of Catalonia in Lleida. She teaches animation in India, where she escapes to whenever she can to draw in her old notebooks, especially at train stations and bus stops. Her films include *Spain I Love You* (1987), *Baquine* (1991), *La Gallina Ciega* (2005), and *Ámár* (2010).

Sketchbook drawings from a trip to India

*"The hand should move by instinct, if such a thing is possible.
I want to see where it takes me."*

DON HERTZFELDT

"I almost always shoot my own animation, so I've never really had to learn the traditional way of providing camera notes for somebody else. I just sort of made up my own shorthand and that's what these are, the numbers and cycles all referring to the order of drawings being shot for each scene. Other numbers in the corners are important notes about the positioning of the camera itself (it's moved around with hand cranks)."

Don Hertzfeldt was born in 1976 in Fremont, California. His animated films have been featured in over 1,000 venues around the world and have collectively received over 150 international awards. Notable honours include a Short Film Palme D'or nomination from the 1999 Cannes Film Festival (*Billy's Balloon*), a 2001 Oscar nomination for Best Animated Short (*Rejected*), the Sundance Film Festival's Jury Award in Short Filmmaking (*Everything Will Be OK*), and Best Picture and Best Screenplay from the Fargo Film Festival (*I Am So Proud of You*). In 2010, Hertzfeldt received the San Francisco International Film Festival's Persistence of Vision Lifetime Achievement Award at the age of 33. His latest film, *It's Such a Beautiful Day*, is the third and final chapter in the *Everything Will Be OK* trilogy. Hertzfeldt lives in Austin, Texas.

ABOVE Film still from *I Am So Proud of You*, 2008 OPPOSITE Corresponding camera notes from *I Am So Proud of You*

"It gets a little more complicated during shots with multiple windows of action going on, like the shot of the clouds in I Am So Proud of You (below). I think there were maybe a dozen or so separate clouds in there, moving in different directions. I'd shoot one set of clouds moving in the far northwest corner of the frame, then close up the camera, rewind the film to the right spot, and then shoot the next set somewhere else with that previous corner blacked out...and you go back and forth on the film strip like that—in this case a dozen or so times— carefully burning each element into the right place in the frame. So this sketch for the cloud scene is more or less me trying to keep track of what I'd already shot."

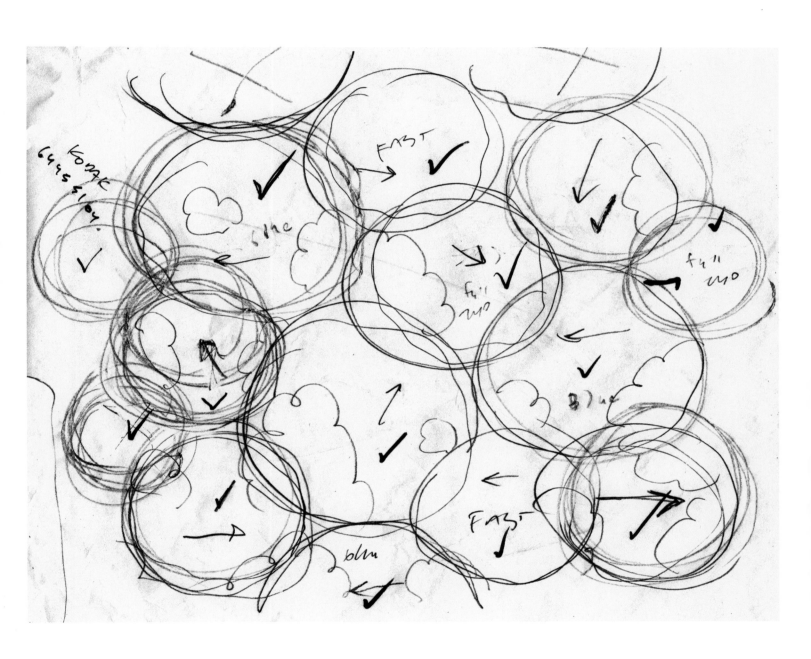

"The films were all shot on an old 35 mm acme rostrum camera pointed down at the artwork. Every shot and special effect was captured in-camera. Most of the scenes in the three films about Bill were shot through strange holes that move around. Looking at the camera notes (below), you'll usually find a sketch of a scene that's surrounded by a heavily scribbled circle of where the hole should frame the animation. I tore little holes in construction paper until I found one that looked good and fitted just right. The floor of the studio during the making of one of these movies was always littered with piles of black construction paper scraps, like some depressed kid's arts and crafts room."

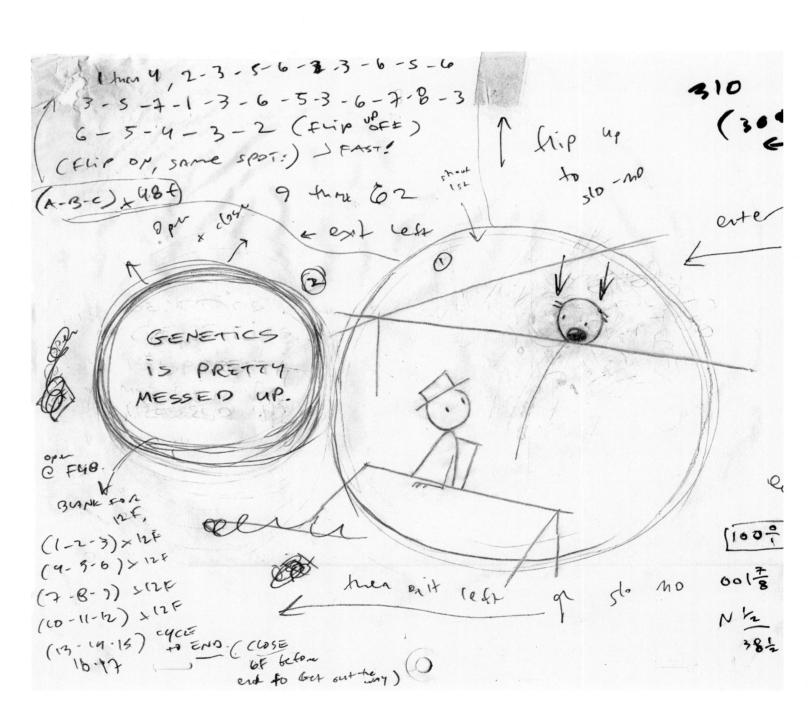

"For this shot of Bill imagining himself on his deathbed in I Am So Proud of You (below) what seems like a pretty straightforward set-up is surrounded by all sorts of scribbly camera notes and reminders. It's a very long shot, with offscreen sunset colors shifting and moving throughout the entire take (little scraps of theatrical color gels that were stop-motion animated off-screen in front of the camera lights). There's a few notes referring to the sunset (red—black—violet colors slowly setting), notes referring to the animated letters that appear midway through, as well as a reminder to blur the corners of the circle-shaped frame with vaseline (via a clear cel taped beneath the lens)."

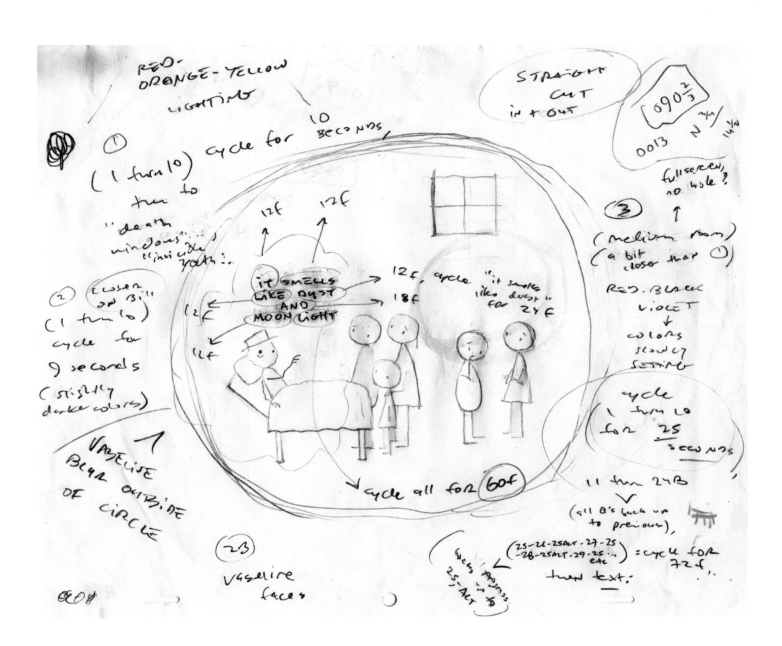

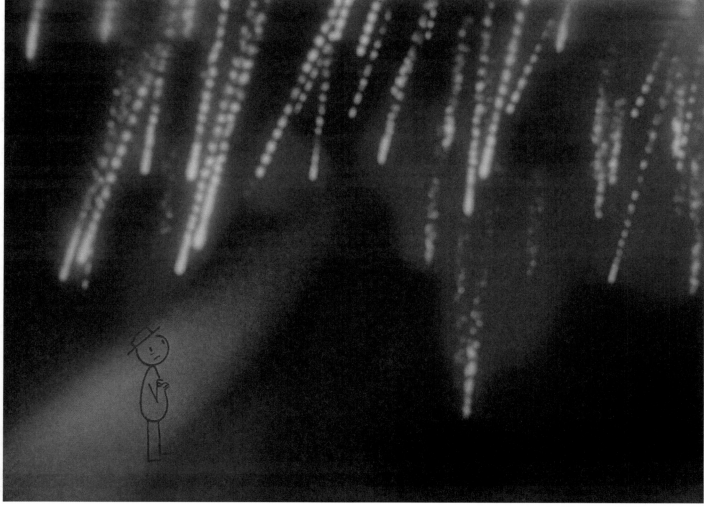

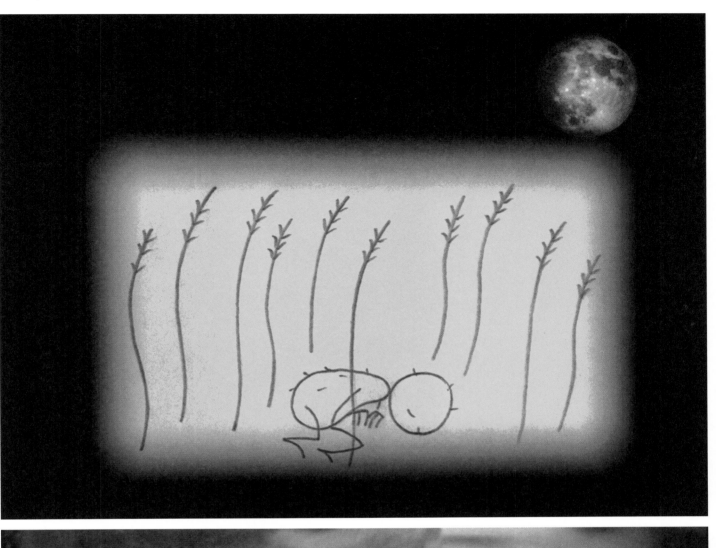

STEPHEN HILLENBURG

Stephen Hillenburg is the creator and executive producer of *SpongeBob SquarePants*, one of Nickelodeon's most popular animated series. Hillenburg's feature film, *The SpongeBob SquarePants Movie*, debuted on November 19, 2004.

Hillenburg graduated from the California Institute of the Arts with a master's degree in experimental animation in 1992. His undergraduate degree, from Humboldt State University, was in natural science with an emphasis on marine biology. Prior to becoming a filmmaker, Hillenburg worked as an exhibit preparator and science educator for kids. By combining these two life-long interests, marine biology and art, he created *SpongeBob SquarePants*.

As a graduate student, Hillenburg made several independent animated films, including *The Green Beret* (1991) and *Wormholes* (1992), which have been exhibited internationally in such festivals as Annecy, Hiroshima, Ottawa, Oberhausen, and the Los Angeles Animation Celebration.

His hobbies include surfing and playing really bad music with his friends.

Animation Diary

The following drawings are from a film I made in 1991–1992 called *Animation Diary*. The objective was to draw one drawing a day for a year. The final animation would consist of 365 drawings and would be shot in consecutive order according to date. I intended to have each drawing express something from each day. I began drawing on January 1, 1991 and ended on December 31, 1991. My thought was that the film would be a visual expression of that year, a visual heartbeat. For this project I made a notebook that could be converted into a light table (this was before the era of laptops).

Drawing 1 Since this was a diary I thought I should open with a self-portrait. You can see the diary notebook on the table in the foreground. I would most often draw at the end of each day.

Drawing 2 Three days later the Gulf War began. The two eyeballs are all that is left of the self-portrait.

Drawing 2

3.5.1991

64

Drawing 3 Iraq has surrendered. It was beginning to rain that week, so I drew a cloud of war machines.

Drawing 4 Of course I would travel with the animation notebook. Here is a drawing from inside a Volkswagen bus. We are about to run out of gas in Cleveland.

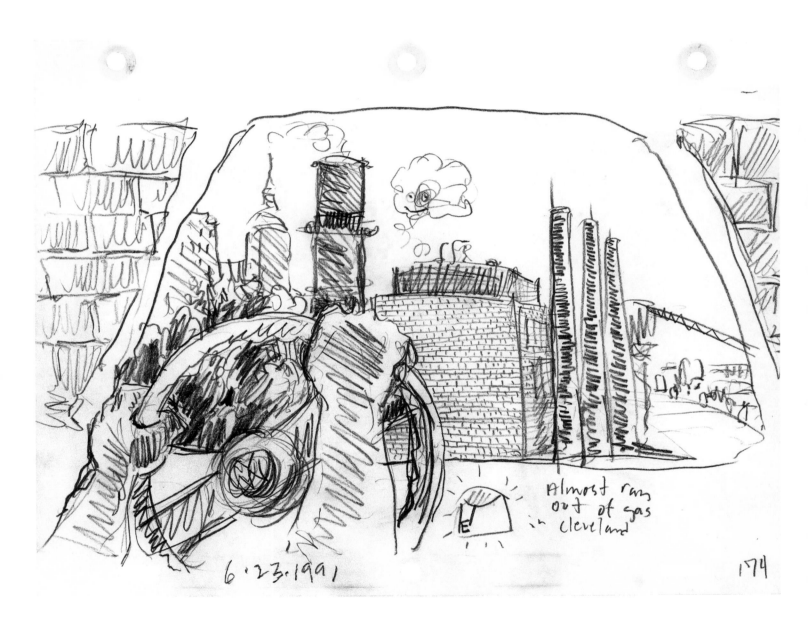

6·23·1991

Almost ran
out of gas
in Cleveland

174

Drawing 5 I made this drawing while flying on an airplane. Pulling a customized notebook equipped with wires and a battery pack out of a bag on an airplane is unthinkable today. Even in 1991 it was an odd sight. The woman sitting next to me seemed visibly nervous.

Drawing 6 Not all of the drawings in the film are literal. Often I would find myself making a transition or an "in between" and still trying to incorporate some memory from that day, like a funny haircut or a raven flying with an orange in its beak.

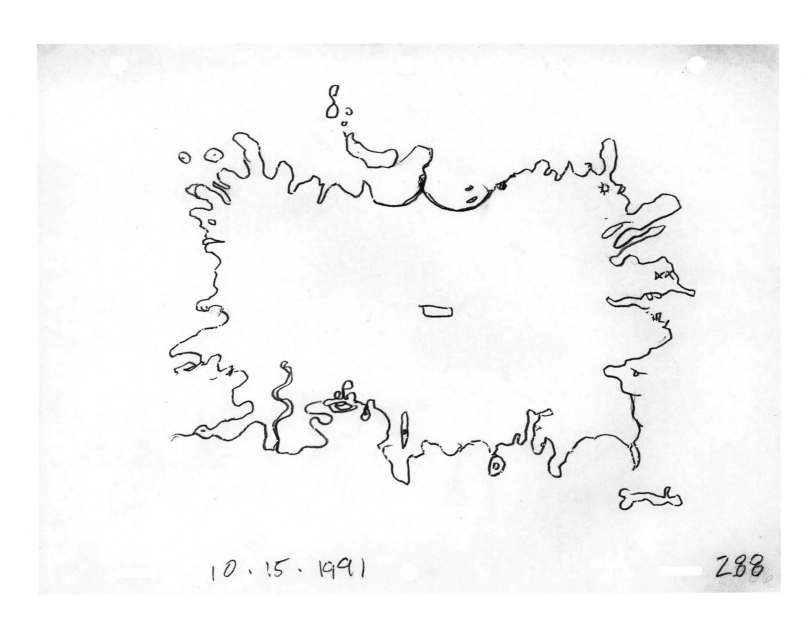

10 · 15 · 1991

288

CHRIS HINTON

"I always work in the privacy of my studio when playing with ideas. It's a very insular, reflective, quiet, personal time. Without question, my ideas spring from the close environment that surrounds me, family mostly, but also friends, social observations, etc. Small events and curiosities are a delight to exploit and expand into film ideas. The smaller the better. The idea of turning some pea-brained insignificant atom into a monument is very appealing."

Born in Galt (now Cambridge), Ontario, in 1952, Chris Hinton has been making animated films for over 40 years. Twice nominated for an Oscar, he has worked as a director for the National Film Board of Canada, the CBC, and several independent animation studios. Hinton has animated, written, directed, and produced over a dozen NFB films, including *Blowhard* (1978), *Lady Frances Simpson* (1978), *Giordano* (1985), Oscar-nominated *Blackfly* (1991), *Watching TV* (1994), *Flux* (2002), and *cNote* (2004). As an independent filmmaker, he has animated and directed *A Nice Day in the Country* (1988) and the Oscar-nominated *Nibbles* (2003). His early work plays with traditional animation design, but moves into the raw and childlike imagery of *Flux*, and later abstraction in *cNote*, a collaboration with contemporary music composer Michael Oesterle. Hinton is currently animating, farming, and playing the fiddle in the countryside of the Eastern Townships of Quebec, Canada.

OPPOSITE Tea time test for *Flux* ABOVE An early color test for *Flux*, painted and drawn on cel

"When I'm actually in production, I work as energetically as I can. I try to work with the enthusiasm and care of a young child. I can always edit later, change colours, etc., so the key for me is not being too self-critical during the process. Having the idea solidly researched is key at this point because it's too easy to lose sight of the original intent. I risk losing confidence if I don't have graphic references of the idea and treatment nearby."

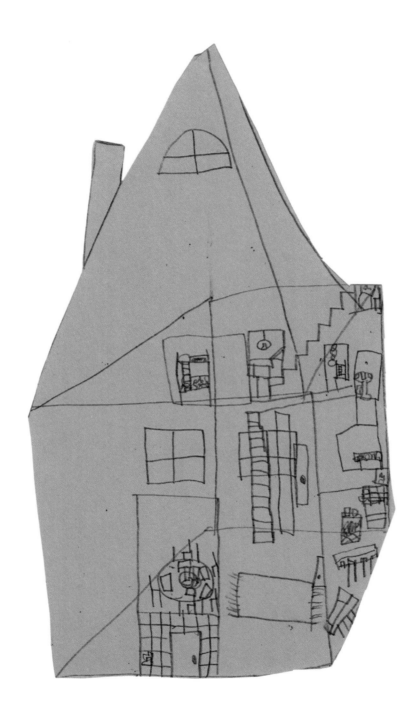

ABOVE Playing with architectural spaces for *Flux*
OPPOSITE Early landscape watercolor for *Flux*

JONATHAN HODGSON

"I've recently completed an animated documentary for BBC2 about people in relationship counseling. The idea was to hide the identities of the contributors by creating animated characters that were quite dissimilar to the real people. Finding the right faces and bodies to sit comfortably with the personalities taking part in the film was a slow and sometimes arduous process. I needed faces that were believable, archetypes rather than stereotypes or caricatures, real-looking characters, not too handsome, but not too ghastly either. I set out hunting for faces in quite a random way, but drawing on the underground seemed to work best. There's almost nowhere else that a total stranger would come and sit face to face with you and there is such a fast turnover of sitters. I also like the expressionistic effect that the lurching motion of the train has on my drawings, forcing a degree of inaccuracy. Most of the main characters in the film came from tube [underground] drawings and all of the drawings I have contributed to this book came from sketchbooks relating to the documentary film."

Jonathan Hodgson was born in Oxford in 1960 and graduated from the Royal College of Art in London in 1985. His first professional commission was to co-direct an animated short about nuclear disarmament for the United Nations with fellow graduate Susan Young. He went on to become a director at Felix Films, a founder member of Bermuda Shorts, and a director at Speedy Films before setting up Sherbet with producer Jonathan Bairstow in 1996. At Sherbet he directed numerous high profile advertising campaigns including Saab, Bell Atlantic, United Bank of Switzerland, and the Home Office. In 2003 he set up Hodgson Films as an outlet for his personal work and continues to be represented by Sherbet for commercials. In 2005 he was featured on the BBC4 documentary series "Animation Nation." In 2007 he worked as an art director on the animated TV series *Charlie and Lola*, and the following year was animation director on Franny Armstrong's groundbreaking documentary feature *The Age of Stupid*. His short films include *Feeling My Way* (1997), BAFTA winning *The Man with the Beautiful Eyes* (1999), BAFTA nominated *Camouflage* (2001), and *Forest Murmurs* (2006). In 2011 Hodgson directed the animation for the first full-length animated documentary for BBC2, *Wonderland: The Trouble with Love and Sex* with director Zac Beattie and producer Jonathan Bairstow of Sherbet. In 2008 he became the program leader for the new BA in Animation at Middlesex University. He lives and works in London.

<small>OPPOSITE</small> Sketchbook drawings made while working on *Wonderland: The Trouble with Love and Sex*, 2011. Many of these were drawn while riding the tube <small>ABOVE</small> Film stills from *Wonderland: The Trouble with Love and Sex*, 2011

"It fits into my pocket and it's worth its weight in gold."

Various sketches from the production *Wonderland: The Trouble with Love and Sex*

STEPHEN IRWIN

"I have several sketchbooks and notebooks on the go at the same time. I have one that contains miscellaneous ideas that are not specific to any particular project. This is where most films start their life when random ideas come together.

Once I start a project I also start a new sketchbook. This is where I collect everything to do with the development of the film, including character design, rough storyboards, notes, and reference material. The sketchbooks help keep things organised as I'm usually developing more than one thing at a time, as well as working on commercial projects."

Stephen Irwin was born in St. Helens in the UK and graduated from Central Saint Martins College of Art and Design in London. His film *Moxie* (2011) was awarded the Grand Prize at the Ottawa International Animation Festival and *The Black Dog's Progress* (2008) won the Best Short Film award at the British Animation Awards in 2010. He has received commissions from the UK Film Council and Film London, BBC New Talent, Warp Films, and Animate Projects (Channel 4/Arts Council England). His films have been screened in competitions all over the world, including at Sundance Film Festival, and at film festivals in Annecy, Zagreb, Edinburgh, Ann Arbor, and Clermont-Ferrand. He was named as one of *Animation Magazine*'s Rising Stars of Animation in 2009. Irwin lives and works in London.

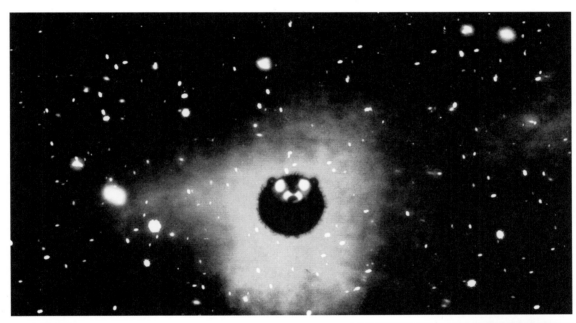

OPPOSITE Early character sketches and story ideas for *Moxie* ABOVE Film stills from *Moxie*, 2011

"I don't particularly keep the books private and I think of them more as workbooks rather than something containing 'personal' work. I'm not sure how much sense they would make to other people anyway as I sometimes have trouble deciphering things I've scribbled late at night myself."

ABOVE Film stills from *Horse Glue*, 2010
OPPOSITE Storyboards for *Horse Glue*

Early layout ideas for *The Black Dog's Progress*

eed at end — on time. New S.H — dancing from
wall — bin outside — side to side — holding
door/window/wall. Home sign — big door/mouth

at dog burn — end with eyes bleed. +FACTORY

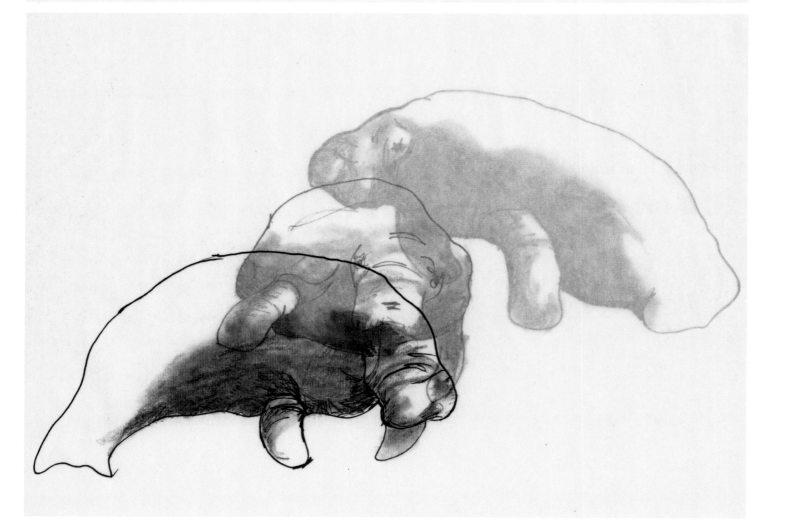

AVISH KHEBREHZADEH

"For each project I find myself challenged by a new motion; for instance, I was working on a new work where two characters were sitting on the back of a rhino and tickling each other to the point that they rolled over and fell on the floor. The intertwined movement of these characters was occupying my mind for a good deal of time before I even started to sketch the entire story. So, sometimes, these movements take over and lead the narration somewhere else. The sketchbook for me is more of a tracking tool to go back to and make sense of the entire narration. I use it only to make sense of my scattered thoughts."

Born in Tehran, Iran in 1969, Avish Khebrehzadeh lives and works in Washington, D.C., and Rome. Khebrehzadeh studied painting in the Accademia di Belle Arti in Rome, photography at the Corcoran College of Art & Design, Washington, D.C., and philosophy at the University of the District of Columbia, Washington, D.C. Her works, lightly drawn and sparingly painted, are compelling in their poetic ambiguity. The contemplative and somewhat mysterious nature of Khebrehzadeh's work allows for a variety of readings and invites viewers' participation through their own imagination. Solo exhibitions of her work have appeared at the Museum of Contemporary Art of Rome (MACRO) and Sprovieri Gallery, London. Khebrehzadeh was included in the 6th Istanbul Biennial (1999), the 5th Liverpool Biennial (2008), and was also a participant in the 50th Venice Biennale in 2003, where she received the Golden Lion Award for the best Young Italian Artist. Other notable exhibitions include The Drawing Room, London; Corcoran Gallery of Art, Washington, D.C.; and the inaugural exhibition of MAXXI (Rome). Khebrehzadeh was included in the New Frontier section of the Sundance Film Festival in 2011, as well as the Innovation section of the Bird's Eye View Film Festival 2011 (London). In 2012 she was a Smithsonian Artist Research Fellow. Her films and installations include *The Unnameable Dream* (animation, 2011) and *Where Do We Go from Here?* (video installation, 2011).

OPPOSITE Film stills from *Solace, So Old, So New*, 2007
ABOVE Photo documentation from the video installation *Solace, So Old, So New*

125

"The drawings included in this book are a timeline created for the film installation piece Solace, So Old, So New (2007). This work consists of three panels installed next to each other. Each panel is a drawing on kozo paper illuminated by a projected video animation which is synchronized with the other two panels. The first panel on the left depicts Nature, the middle panel is House and the right panel is Town Square. All three are in three different times and three different locations with respect to ours.

This was one of the most complex projects that I have done and, in a sense, the hardest to navigate using my usual process (I allowed the story to develop as I was moving forward). So, in order to make sense of what was happening simultaneously in all three scenes, I started to work on an exact timeline development for each channel. Many years ago I had seen a book where Shostakovich was explaining how he started creating music for Eisenstein's movies (I think the book was about the early days of film music). The challenge for him was to remain creative and musical, and at the same time adhere to the timeline dictated by the movie. He had sketches very similar to what you see here: scenes were broken down into small portions and the musical ideas were written for each block of time. I applied the same structure to the three-channel approach: it got really complicated when we started to add the music."

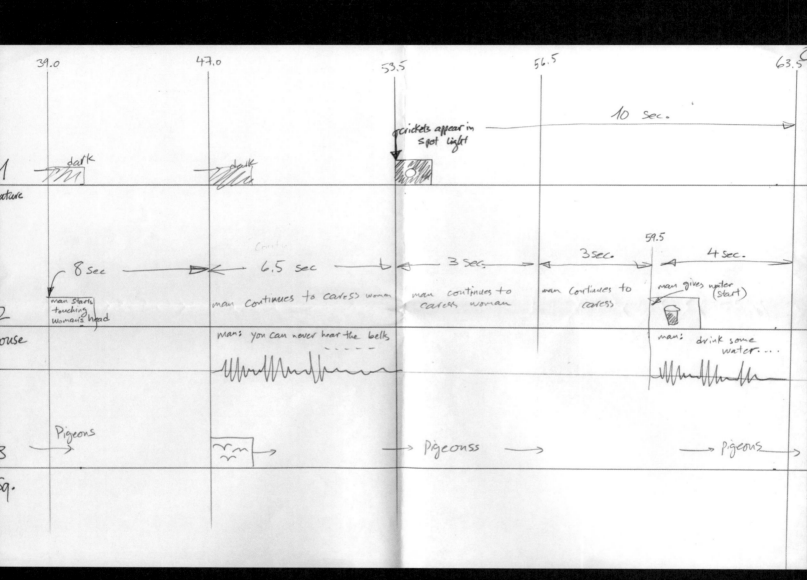

Timeline for *Solace, So Old, So New*

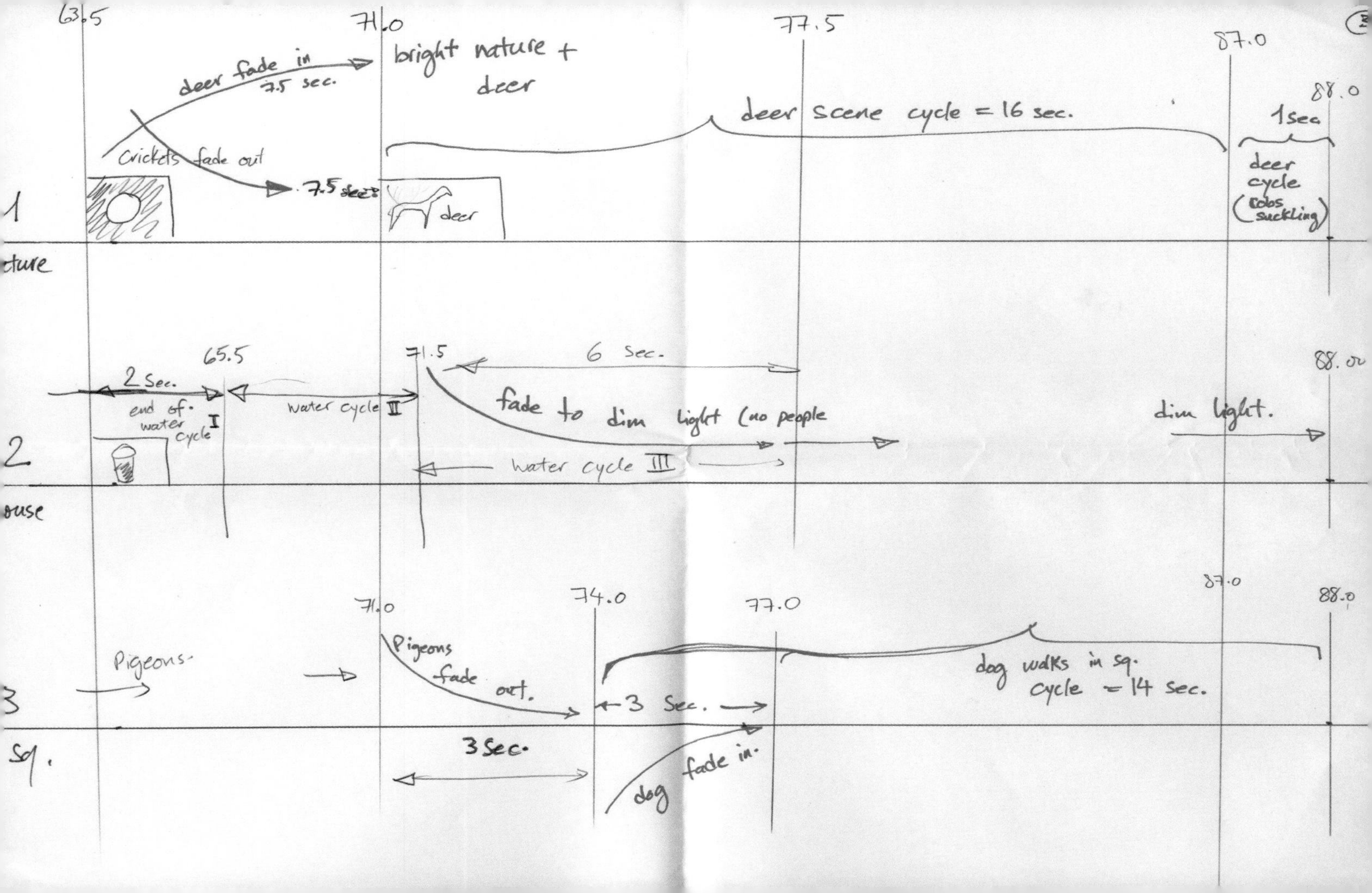
63.5
71.0
77.5
87.0
88.0
deer fade in
7.5 sec.
bright nature +
deer
deer scene cycle = 16 sec.
1sec
crickets fade out
7.5 sec.
deer
deer cycle
(cobs suckling)
1
cture
65.5
71.5
6 sec.
88.00
2 sec.
end of water cycle I
water cycle II
fade to dim light (no people
dim light.
water cycle III
2
ouse
87.0
88.0
71.0
74.0
77.0
Pigeons.
Pigeons fade out.
dog walks in sq.
cycle = 14 sec.
3 Sec.
3
sq.
3 sec.
dog fade in.

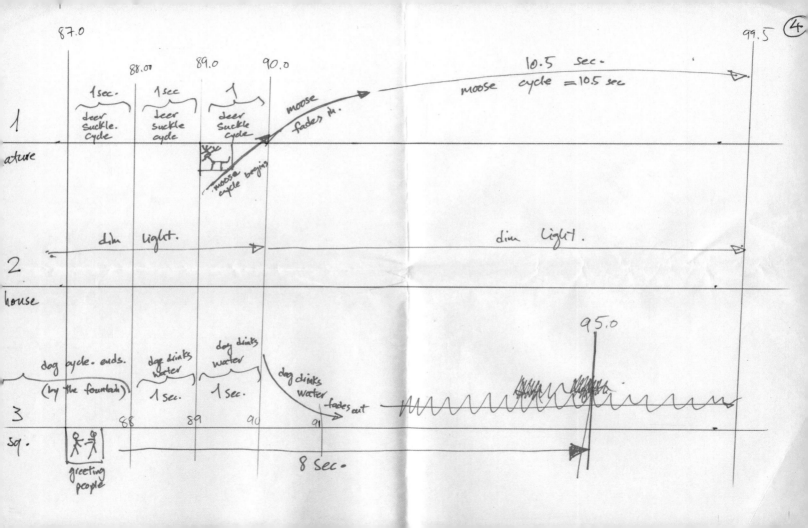

87.0   99.5 ④

88.0   89.0   90.0   10.5 sec.

1

1 sec. 1 sec 1   moose   moose cycle = 10.5 sec
deer   deer   deer fades in.
suckle. suckle suckle
cycle   cycle   cycle

ature

moose begins cycle

2

dim light.   dim light.

house

3 dog cycle. ends. dog drinks dog drinks   95.0
   (by the fountain) water   water
           1 sec.   1 sec. dog drinks
                    water
        88   89   90 91 fades out

sq. greeting people   8 sec.

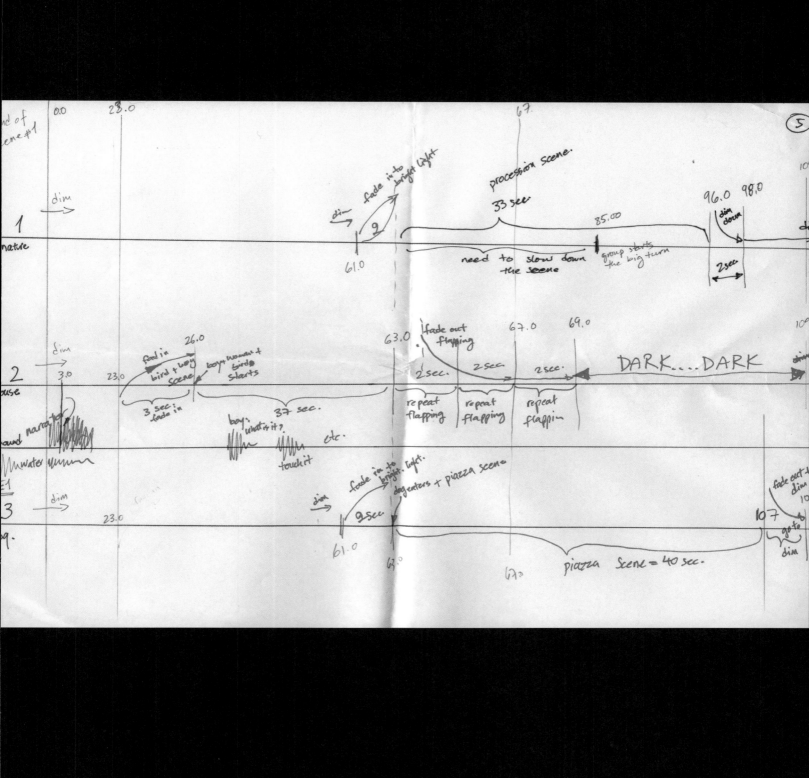

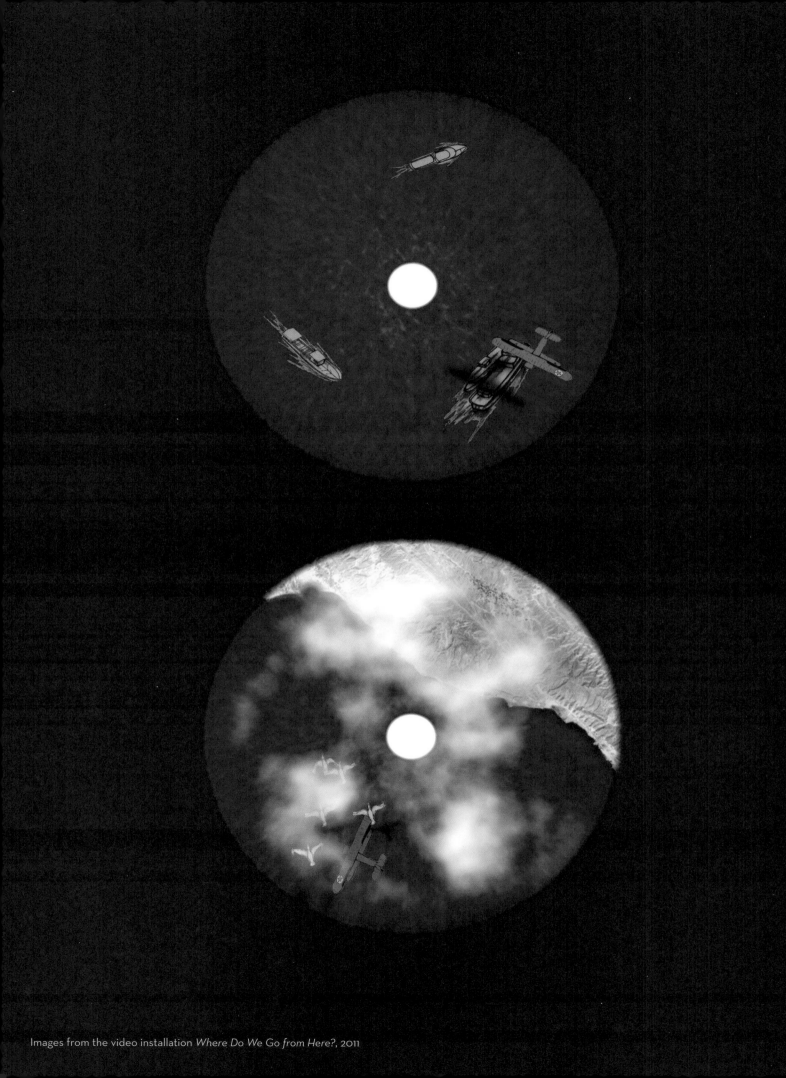

Images from the video installation *Where Do We Go from Here?*, 2011

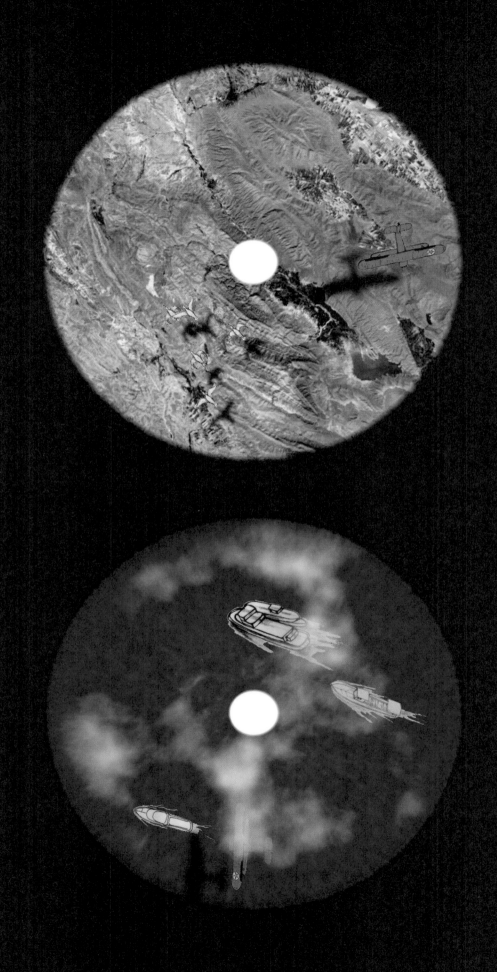

FRAN KRAUSE

"I like drawing very small, and with messy media—it leaves a lot to chance and gives me challenges along the way. I heard that Hitchcock thought the whole process of filmmaking was boring after he'd figured out storyboards. He already knew how the film was going to turn out! I don't want to work that way. Just like the audience, I want to be excited and curious right up until the end."

Fran Krause was born in Utica, New York. In 1999, while studying for a masters at the Rhode Island School of Design, he made the award-winning *Mister Smile*. After graduating, he started working at Nickelodeon on *Blue's* *Clues* (2000). He lived in New York for 10 years and worked as a freelance animator, animating segments for *Saturday Night Live*, and working on projects such as *Little Einsteins* (2005–06) and *SuperJail* (2008). He collaborated with his brother Will to make two pilots for Cartoon Network: *Utica Cartoon* (2001) and *The Upstate Four* (2007). His recent films include *Rooftop Signal Film* (2008), *Dog in the Burning Building* (2010), and *Nosy Bear* (2011). He currently lives in Los Angeles and teaches in the Character Animation program at CalArts, Valencia, California.

Sketchbook drawings

*"These are sketches from 2010 to 2011, when I was
making my film Nosy Bear. I made the art for the film
entirely in my sketchbook because I wanted to stay away
from the computer as much as I could. I like fiddling with
computers, but I also feel that they can be 'sticky,' in that
their style can stick to mine, and change it in ways that
I don't always like. Also, it makes me feel more alive to
be outside and away from my desk. Like I'm playing hooky
but still getting work done."*

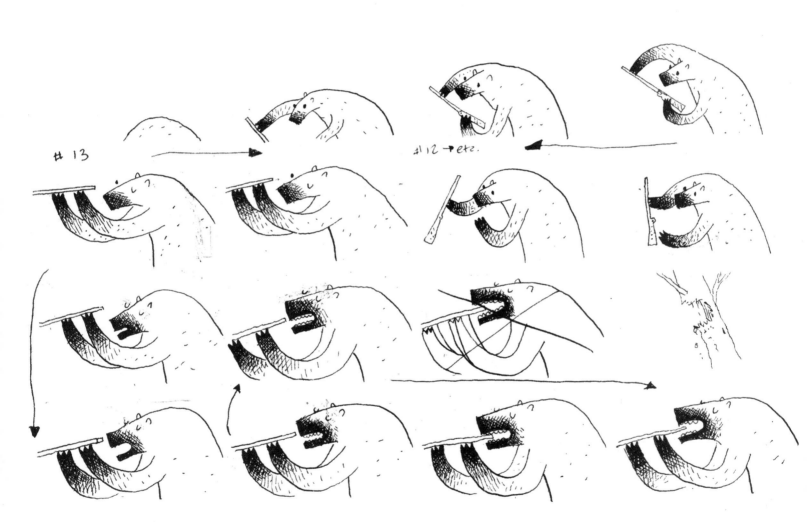

ABOVE AND OPPOSITE Sketchbook drawings/final drawings used for *Nosy Bear*
PAGES 136–37 Sketchbook drawings

"I think of my sketchbook as a place outside of my head in which to put ideas. It's the only book I can plagiarize!"

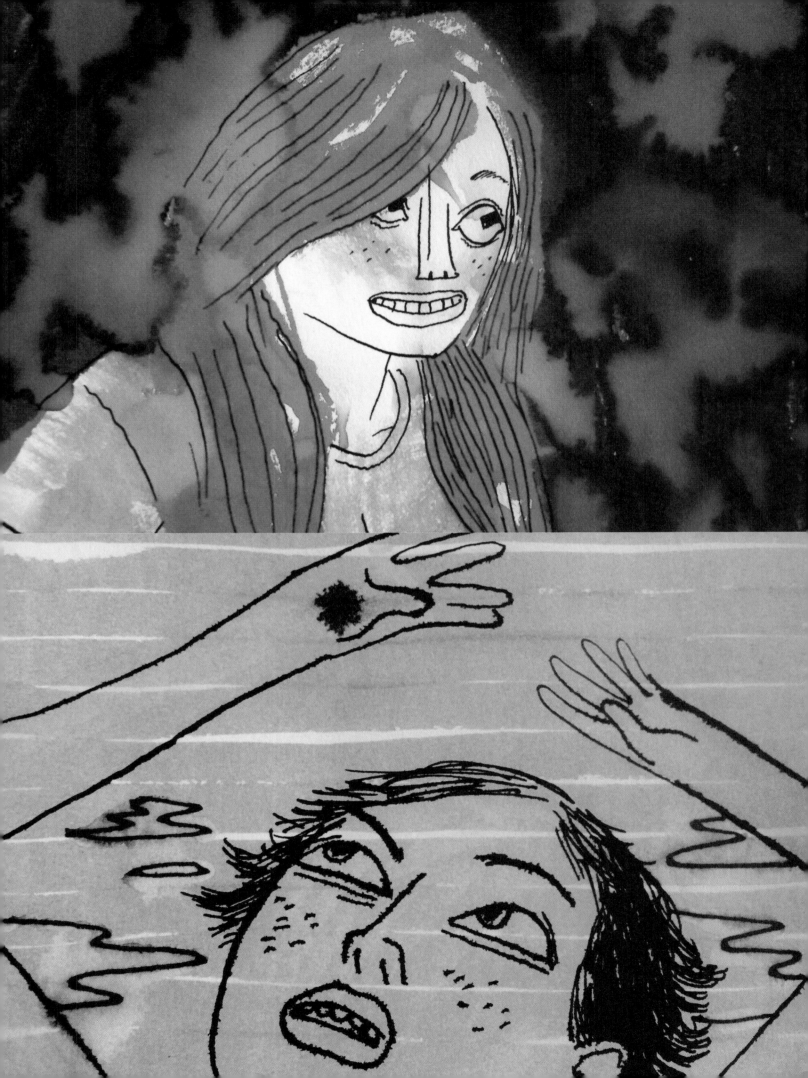

RAIMUND KRUMME

"When I start animating a movement I try and perceive the motion as a whole, and I will draw this Gestalt before I start to deconstruct it and concentrate on the different fragments in the movement. Reliving that movement with the hand after observation might not show the exact succession of shifting particles from one location to another, but rather an idea of that movement."

Raimund Krumme was born in Cologne, Germany in 1950. He has been making animated films since the 1980s and commercials since the mid-1990s. His films include *Seiltänzer* (*Rope Dancer*, 1986), *Die Kreuzung* (*The Crossroads*, 1991), *Passage* (1994), *The Message* (2000), and *Der Gefangenenchor* (*The Chorus*, 2004). He has taught at art schools and universities in both the US and Europe, including CalArts, Valencia, California, the Academy for Television in Halle, Germany, and since 2006 at the Academy of Media Arts in Cologne.

Moodboard and sketches for *Lost Ones*, 2011

wie gehen d. Charaktes?

"As in drawing a single image, parts are ignored, others are exaggerated. On a good day drawing becomes dance. Movement matters for itself."

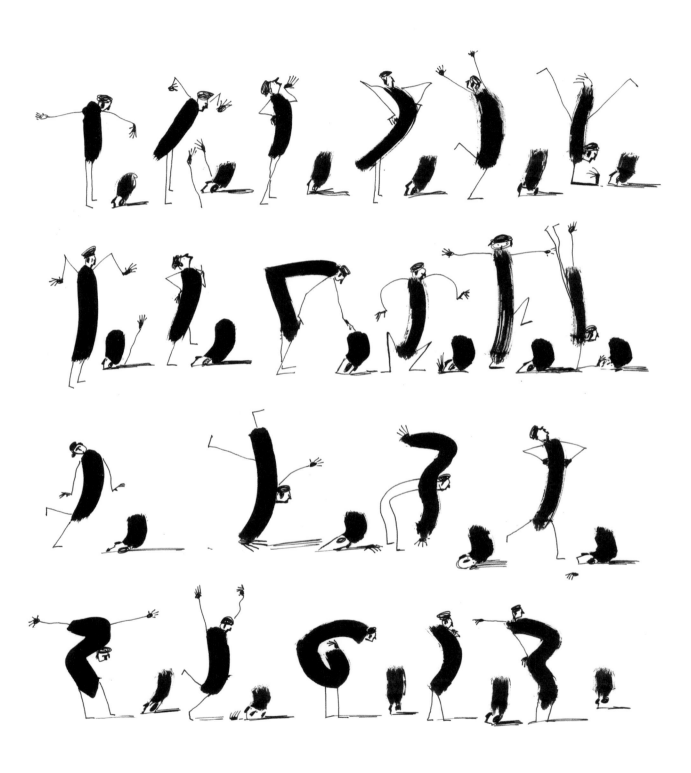

OPPOSITE A study on movement of characters walking and
also movement of body masses
ABOVE Sketches for the film _Passage_, developed from
rough ink brushstrokes

141

SIMONE MASSI

"The ideas for my work are often based on tiny things that are difficult to describe: glances, gestures... Something that I saw or dreamt and in some way touched my soul. If, over the years, these memories become monumental, it means it is time to take them out and tell them in the form of an animated poem."

Simone Massi was born in Pergola, Italy in 1970. He was a factory worker until he left for art school in Urbino where he received his degree in Animated Cinema. He lives and works in Italy where he has completed 15 independent award-winning films including *Io So Chi Sono* (*I Know Who I Am*, 2004), *La memoria dei cani* (*The Memories of Dogs*, 2006), *Nuvole, mani* (*Clouds, Hands*, 2009), and *Dell'ammazzare il maiale* (*About Killing the Pig*, 2011).

Sketches for *La memoria dei cani (The Memories of Dogs)*, 2006

"NUVOLE MANI" Storyboard 1Ø aprile 2008

		Camera	Durata	Suono	Status	Cartelle/Scansioni	Riferimenti
	1 MANI DEL PADRE	FERMO ZOOM–		(Fabbrica)	OK	origin 20 2009/01 0001–0389 (01–03 ciclo?) (387-389 ciclo?)	
	2 ESCE NERO (prima guarda in basso)	ZOOM–	50"	Campanelli? (pernacchio)	OK		
	2 MANI DELLA MADRE	ZOOM– FERMO	(1'00")	Foglie mosse che scorr. strada Lamiera che sbatte (cigolii)	OK	marzo 2009/02 2a (0390–0646) 2c (390 nero ciclo)	
	3 SI ALLONTANA PORTA DELLA CASA CHE SBATTE – NERO (Una foglia che vola poi di più e la porta che sbatte)	ZOOM–	50"	Vento, foglie Porta che sbatte	OK	2b (002–73) 2c (01–72) (72 nero ciclo)	
	4 TRONCHI NERO SCOSTA IL NERO?	ZOOM–	10" (2'00")	Taglio del bosco	OK	marzo 2009/03 3a (001–123) 124–156 (124-156) 3a (157–217)	Zeta/Centr/bosco/zoom 1→78
	5 RAGAZZO CAMMINA (ogni tanto muove la testa, nello strisciare contro i rami)	ZOOM–	40"	Taglio del bosco	OK	3b (001–172)	Zeta/Centr/camUNG 50-68 Zeta/Centr/completo 15, 26 Zeta/Centr/Bosco/8 o? Graffi 1 o 2 Zeta/Centr/Bosco/zoom 1
	6 SI FERMA SBOCCIA ARANCIO	FERMO PANORAMICA ↓		Taglio del bosco	OK		
	7 SVIENE	ZOOM–	35" (3'00")	Albero cade	OK	marzo 2009/04 04a (001–300) (300 bianco ciclo)	Zeta/Centr/Caduta 12X
	8 CADONO VESTITI Bosco Capovolto	FERMO		Poesia	OK	Prove/Finale 1 (000–171) 9a (34–161 2 volte) (162-162c ciclo)	Zeta/Centr/bosco/35 finale?
	9 CADONO Alberi, Cielo e Nuvole	FERMO		Poesia	OK		Zeta/Nuvole/senza Tit. 1
	10 A TERRA STRACCI (L'UOMO) Nuvole/Lumaca sul dito	FERMO		Silenzio	OK	2 (172–259) 2 volte	Zeta/Nuvole 1,2,3
	11 SI SVEGLIA, SI VOLTA	ZOOM–		Rum. Ambiente	OK	05 bosco/01 sveglia 05 bosco/05 sialza/02 05 bosco/06 cane/dist cattura X 155 Dist cattura x 19 ritira stecca x 53	
	12 DI FRONTE C'È UN CANE…	ZOOM–	(4'00")	Musica	OK	3 (10–87) 2 volte Zoom, terra, nero (21 zoom 22-45)	Zeta/Centr/bosco/zoom 96–104 FINE zoom 62–67
	13 SI VOLTA, CAMMINA SI COLORA DI GIALLO (COMPARE IL RAGAZZO)	ZOOM–	5"	Musica	OK	4 (1–21) 2 volte (8–10 ciclo) (21 bianco ciclo)	06 cane fronte 1/229→325
	14 RAGAZZO GIALLO SI TOCCA, ANNUSA (TESTA = FUMO)	ZOOM–	5"		O	5 (01–60) 2 volte 5 Vasche Def/com (1–12) 2 volte 5 vasche Def/Org (13–49) 2 volte	
	15 RAGAZZO = CASA SCENDONO PANNI Panni	ZOOM–		Vento Voci al fiume	O		Zeta/Panni 2
	16 PANNI = CAPELLI (CASA SCOMPARE) Panni e vaschette	ZOOM–		lo chiamano "Simonee!"	OK	6 (2060–2098) 2 volte? 6 2098b (2099–2426) ciclo, ripetere 2 volte 6 (2099–2173) 2 volte? 6 Finale Alter (2174–2223) 2221-2223 ciclo	
	17 RAGAZZO ANNUSA ENTRA VASCHETTA Vaschette	ZOOM–		Campanelli Acqua	OK	6 2209 (00–26) 24-26 ciclo	
	18 CA PRENDE	FERMO	13"	Campanelli Acqua	OK		
	19 LA DA A BERE AL CANE ALZA IL CAPO (Il ragazzo guarda giù (o a lato o giù su))	PANORAMICA ↓	6"	Rum. Ambiente	OK	Il ragazzo guarda...	
	20 NUVOLE (cane alza la testa, ragazzo guarda in su)	STACCO	15"	Silenzio (Musica?)	O	7 (1–40) 2 volte	Zeta/Nuvole/Senza Tit 2 -04,05,06

da correggere: CANE SI VOLTA E BEVE IN RITARDO (RISPETTO AL MOVIM. DELL'CORPO) CICLO VASCHETTE

"Often, ideas come when I'm not ready: when I'm travelling on a train or at night, just before I fall asleep. I quickly search for a piece of paper and pour all these thoughts down..."

OPPOSITE Storyboard for *Nuvole, mani (Clouds, Hands)* ABOVE Color tests for *Nuvole, mani (Clouds, Hands)*

"Once I have the story I begin to sketch, and in a few days I have a storyboard. But for me, my storyboards are ever-changing maps, as I never follow the original route in its entirety. I need years to make a film and, for me, the story will move and change in that time. New words and ideas will come to fill my train trips and sleepless nights: the storyboard will be changed dozens of times."

ABOVE Film still from *Nuvole, mani (Clouds, Hands)*, 2009
OPPOSITE Color tests for *Nuvole, mani (Clouds, Hands)*

Giallo (Blu)

Giallo (

Giallo (verde rosso Blu)

Giallo (ver

Giallo (Verde, Rosso) Blu

Giallo, Blu

MIWA MATREYEK

"I often work in an everything-and-the-kitchen-sink kind of approach. I lay out a bunch of loose ideas and see what works and what doesn't as I combine them together to make the overall structure of the piece. The whole process works like a collage, putting things next to each other until I see a way for everything to fall into place."

Miwa Matreyek was born in Seattle in 1979 and grew up in both Japan and the San Francisco Bay Area. She is an internationally recognized animator, designer, and multimedia artist. She creates animated short films as well as works that integrate animation and live performance/installation via projection. Her animation shorts have been shown at LA Freewaves, San Francisco International Asian American Film Festival, Philadelphia Film Festival, and the Platform International Animation Festival among other places. Her multimedia performance works, *Dreaming of Lucid Living* (2007) and *Myth and*

Infrastructure (2010), have been shown internationally at festivals such as the Sundance Film Festival, TEDGlobal, ISEA, Radar L.A., TBA Festival, Anima Mundi International Animation Festival of Brazil, and the Exploratorium. Her solo video performance, *Dreaming of Lucid Living*, won the Princess Grace Award for Film, as well as the Student Grand Prix and Audience Choice Award for Best Performance/Installation at the Platform International Animation Festival. She is a founding member and core collaborator of the performance media group Cloud Eye Control. Her most recent works include *Under Polaris* (collaborative video performance, Cloud Eye Control, 2009), *Myth and Infrastructure* (solo video performance, 2010), and *Lumerence* (short film, 2012). Matreyek is an MFA graduate from the CalArt's Experimental Animation program (2007). She currently lives and works in Los Angeles.

ABOVE Stills from the solo video performance *Myth and Infrastructure*, 2010 OPPOSITE Ideas for the animated film *Digitopia*, 2005

what is the history of this SOCIETY?

BRAIN SUPER COMPUTER

Telescope: look to the sky
→ imagination distorted the realities of the universe
(→ are humans naturally optimistic or) pessimistic?

CALLING OUT TO ALIEN CIVILIZATIONS.

CULTURE OF THIS FUTURE?
LANGUAGE OF THIS FUTURE?

DIFFERENT CULTURE.
NOT ONLY DOES TECHNOLOGY
CHANGE THE WAY WE LIVE
BUT ALSO THE WAY WE THINK
NANO BOTS to NEUTRALIZE
AGGRESSION. (WAR)

GENESIS.

Electric towers/pylons made out of cats in the cradle
ARMS MOVE TO MAKE NEW CONNECTIONS.

LINK   LINK   LINK

TRANSPORTATION

METRO SYSTEM LIKE ARTERIES.

AUTOMOBILE

NANO TECHNOLOGY REGENERATION

WHAT IS THE PROGRESS FROM PREVIOUS WORKS?

↝ IDEAS // SCENES
↳ BUILD COLLAGES
SEARCH IMAGES
EVERY WEEK.

for image visualization and collection

KEEP HEAD IN VISION, VISION IN HEAD

"Since there are a lot of puzzles and problem-solving in my work, the sketches are a place to ponder an image that I want to create, to figure out how to do it. I also often write out words, phrases, ideas that I find relevant to the project, for future investigation or as motivation, or big manifesto-like claims about what I want my work to be."

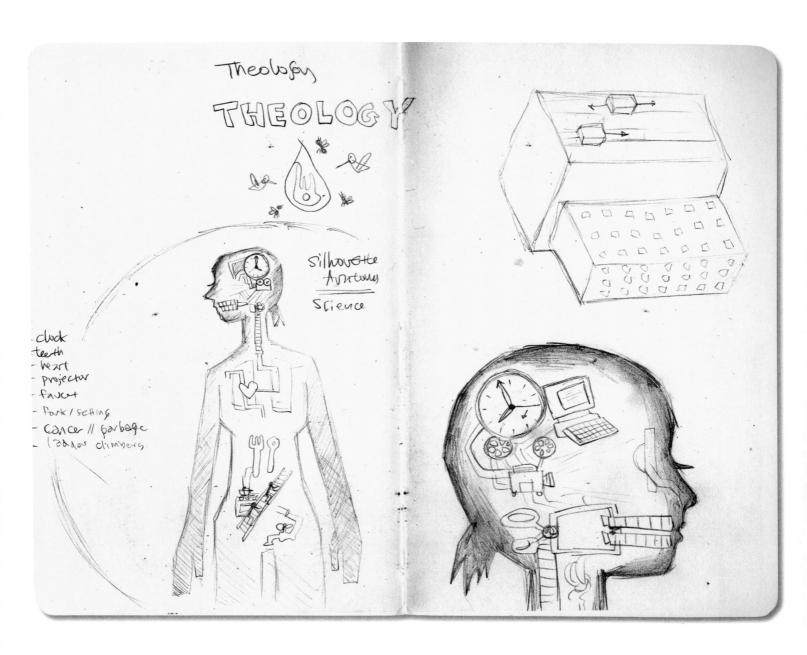

Stills from the solo video performance *Dreaming of Lucid Living*, 2007

FLORENCE MIAILHE

"I like to go back and forth between documentary and the oneiric, the quotidian, and the fantastic. I'm inspired by a story or a place that speaks to me. The two come together the same way that the desire to tell or not to tell a story also comes together, to be as realistic or as abstract as possible. Before each film, I try to start with a series of quick life sketches, before throwing myself into creating the script.

The fact that I work alone, and with such a small set-up, means that I can make changes, add elements to the initial plan, let certain parts be more improvised. The danger of a work that is too thought-out is that I would become merely a technician on my own film. I prefer to be able to continue to create as I go along. The animatic provides me with a path to follow—but along the way I am free to take any shortcuts that crop up."

Florence Miailhe was born in Paris in 1956. She graduated from the National School of Decorative Arts, Paris in 1980. As well as being a painter, she works as an illustrator and a graphic designer for commercial advertising. After a series of exhibitions on the theme of hammams, she directed her first animated film, *Hammam*, in 1991. Her other films include *Shéhérazade* (1995), *Histoire d'un prince devenu borgne et mendiant* (*The Story of a Prince Who Became a One-Eyed Beggar*, 1996), *Les Oiseaux blancs, les oiseaux noirs* (*Black and White Birds*, 2003), *Conte de quartier* (*Urban Tale*, 2006), *Matières à Rêver* (2008), and *Texture of Dreams* (2009). Her films have been broadcast throughout Europe and shown at international festivals, including Clermont-Ferrand, Oberhausen International Short Film Festival, Annecy, London International Film Festival, and Cannes where she won a jury special mention. Miailhe lives and works in Paris.

OPPOSITE Sketches for *Histoire d'un prince devenu borgne et mendiant* (*The Story of a Prince Who Became a One-Eyed Beggar*)
ABOVE Sketches of nudes dancing for personal series

PAGE 156 Research of colored atmospheres for *La Traversée*, a work-in-progress feature-length animated film
PAGE 157 First sketches for the storyboard of *Histoire d'un prince devenu borgne et mendiant* (*The Story of a Prince Who Became a One-Eyed Beggar*)
PAGES 158–59 Film still from *Conte de quartier* (*Urban Tale*), *2006*

③

la table se couvre de mets...
en succession
au tendre
enchaine
idem
pour
les boissons

le portefaix regarde à droite
à gauche, ne sachant plus
où donner de la tête.

Fondu au blanc on se retrouve dans la
chambre de shiérazade il fait jour...

revoir la transition. (?)

Fondu au noir avec la chambre de shiérazade...

Les soeurs amènent
différents mets, boissons
sur la table et
enlèvent au fur et
à mesure leur vêtements
afin d'être plus à l'aise
le portefaix mange et
boit.

puis elles s'installent
confortablement à
côté de lui et tout
trois continuent à boire.
Gros plans sur les veines, les bouches

"mais, tu ne
peux rester avec
nous qu'à la
condition de ne
pas chercher
à savoir ce que
tu ne dois pas
savoir, de peur
d'entendre des
choses que tu
pourrais ne
point aimer !!

Le portefaix était si
heureux qu'il croyait
être dans un rêve.
Ensemble, ils boivent
jusqu'à l'ivresse.

jeux dans l'eau
éclaboussements...

zoom arrière

Le portefaix est
assis nu dans la
piscine les trois
femme se tournent
et le rejoignent sur
le bord. ou
elles s'allongent
jambes écartées
devant le
portefaix.

quand la boisson
se fut emparée
de leur esprit,
les trois dames se
dépouillèrent de
leurs vêtements et
plongèrent dans
la piscine...

dialogues du
portefaix et
des dames
au sujet de
leurs parties
intimes...

MIRAI MIZUE

"My animation is the same as music."

Mirai Mizue was born in 1981 and studied animation at Tama Art University in Tokyo. He creates abstract animated films using cell structure, and geometric and scientific patterns as motifs. His films have been selected for major animation festivals, including Annecy, Ottawa, Zagreb, and Hiroshima. His film *Modern No. 2* (2011) won the Sacem Award for original music at Annecy in 2012 and was nominated for the Orizzonti award at the 68th Venice International Film Festival in 2011. His film *Jam* (2009) was based on a very simple idea: the increasingly varied the sounds, the greater the number of creatures, with the intention of filling the screen with chaotic movements. His other films include *Devour Dinner* (2008), *Modern* (2010), *Playground* (2010), *And, And* (2011), *Tatamp* (2011), and *Timbre A–Z* (2011), 26 short animations based on the letters of the alphabet made in 26 days. On 1 April 2012 he began *Wonder 365 Animation Project* for which he planned to draw and upload one second of abstract animation every day for a year. He is a co-founder and co-organizer of CALF, an independent distributor of new Japanese abstract and experimental animation, and has released a DVD collection of his work under this label. He is a board member of the Association of Japanese Animations and a member of ASIFA Japan. Mizue lives and works in Tokyo.

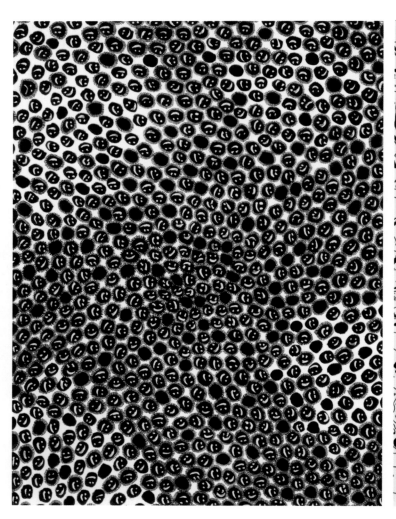

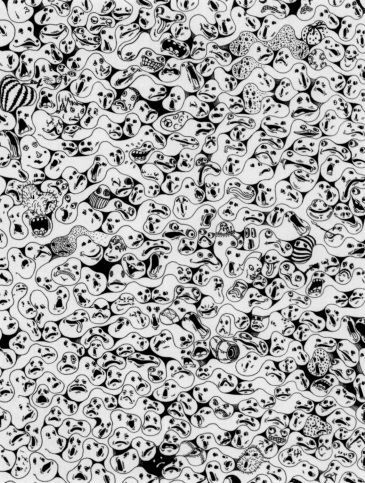

ABOVE Sketchbook drawings OPPOSITE Book cover image for a collection of short stories by Yasutaka Tsutsui

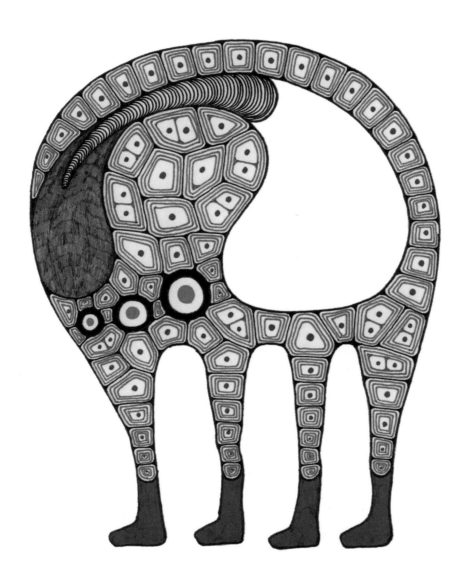

ABOVE Image from the film *Devour Dinner*
OPPOSITE Sketchbook drawing

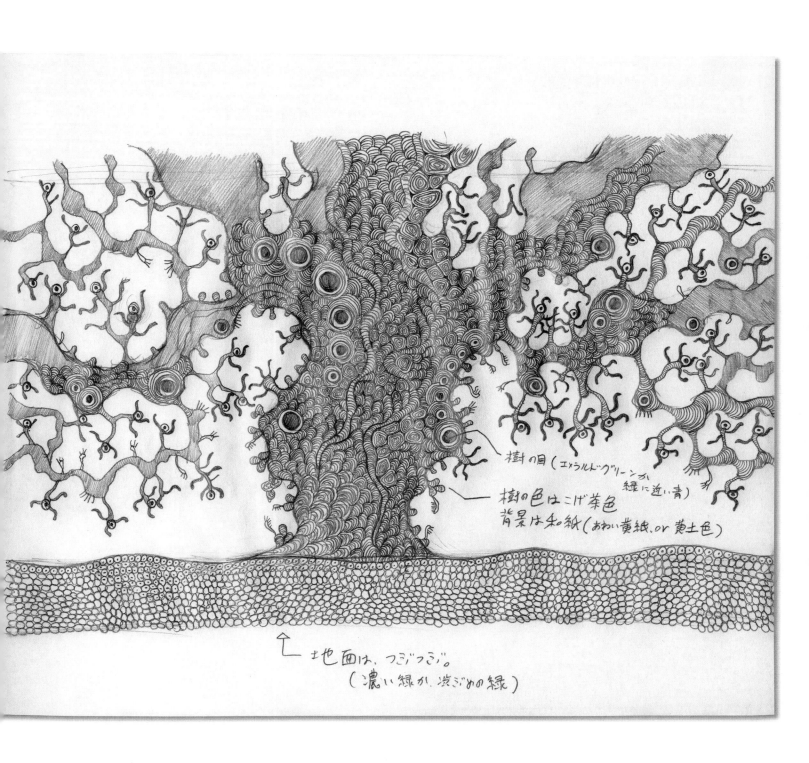

樹の目 (エメラルドグリーンが
　　　緑に近い青)

樹の色はこげ茶色
背景は和紙 (あわい黄紙, or 黄土色)

↑ 地面は, つぶつぶ。
　(濃い緑か, 渋ごめの緑)

OPPOSITE Sketchbook drawing
ABOVE Image for *Shimajiro's WOW!*, a children's TV program

DAVID OREILLY

"These lists represent about six months of production on my animated short film The External World*. These pages are practically the only physical evidence of my filmmaking process. I like to keep almost every task involved in the production on the computer, including development and design, which is usually done on paper. I feel that designing inside the software itself is much more in harmony with the medium of 3D and works to its strengths, even though I love drawing."* [1]

David OReilly was born in Kilkenny, Ireland, in 1985 and is now based in Berlin. At the age of 15 he began working as an assistant at local animation studios, teaching himself 3D software in his spare time. He has amassed a cult following with his unique and engrossing short films, *Please Say Something* (2009) and *The External World* (2010), which premiered at the 67th Venice International Film Festival and Sundance Film Festival. He has won many awards: a Grand Prix at Ottawa International Animation Festival, a Golden Bear for Best Short film: *Berlinale* (2009), The Cartoon d'Or (2009), a Golden Zagreb Award at Zagreb Animafest (2010), and a Grand Prix at the Stuttgart International Festival of Animated Film (2011). He keeps up a blog about low-tech 3D CGI work, www.lowend3D.com, and after many years in Berlin, Germany, he currently lives and works in Los Angeles.

ABOVE Film still from *The External World*, 2010 OPPOSITE AND PAGES 168–71 To-do lists for the production of *The External World*, 2010

1 Sited on www.davidoreilly.com

27 JUNE

FINAL ANIMATIC SHIT

1. OLD FOLKS MUSIC + EXTEND
2. DOOR OPEN SOUND SITCOM
3. EXTEND PAPA SFX GATEAU
4. SHIT RUN BG SFX BRING BACK
5. BRING UP PACHELBEL
6. PIANO FISH VIDEO CUTS TOO EARLY?
7. CAR EXPLO SFX TIMING
8. MARIO BRICK UP SFX SYNC
9. SFX SQUEAKS CUT OFF
10. BIRD SFX
11. BRING BACK HOSPITAL MUSIC
12. AFX - TRANSITION TO BLACK AFTER TRAIN HIT

25 JUNE

1. RERENDER HAPPY GUY PHARMACY
2. RERENDER HAPPY GUY DOCTOR
3. RENDER HAPPY GUY KNOCK DOWN FERRET NEW
4. ADD NEWLY RENDERED SCENES TO EDIT
5. ALIGN ALL NEW SHOTS + RENDER
6. ADD FEMALE VERSION OF "PAPA! NO!"
7. RENDER NEW SITCOM
8. COMPOSITE NEW SITCOM + DROP IN EDIT
9. WATCH ANIMATIC THROUGH
10. RERENDER ICECREAM WITH EARLIER DISTORT
11. RENDER NEW RABBIT SILHOUETTE
12. RENDER HEAD PALE

25TH JUNE

ANIMATIC FIXES

1. CARS / TRAIN IN OPENING
2. EYES OVER SLEEPING CHARS
3. SFX FRM AFTER CRAMP
4. LOUDER THUMP
5. RACHEL BG A BIT LIGHTER
6. GREEN OVER HAPPY GUY?
7. COIN INSERT SOUND EFFECT FRM CHANGE NOISE
8. BLACK FRAME AFTER NO POLE EFFECT LINE
9. CAMERA SFX + FLASHES ON ART GALLERY + APPROVING CLAPS
10. MOUTH SHAPES OVER TOY SFX
11. SECOND "OW".. AS BOX HIT BY GHOST HAND
12. ADD REAL TISSUE ON TISSUE BOX
13. ADAM AS POLICE OFFICER
14. MAKE COP EXPLODE
15. UNACCEPTABLE WRITING! STEREO.
16. GET MAX NEW FIRE ALARM AUDIO

17. MAKE FOUNTAIN OF BLOOD ON TUB GIRL (SHOWER)
18. FIX HAPPY GUY EYES
19. FIX HAPPY GUY BUTT WASH TIME
20. GRANDAD OPEN + CLOSE SOUNDS
21. FRAME OF ANIMATIC ON HOSPITAL SCN
22. STEREOISE CUTE CHARS TERRA
23. MAKE AUDIENCE THEME SOUND FRAME
24. DRAMATIC CLASSICAL MUSIC TO HOSPITAL SERIAL

JBMPO389984YY
2E0

25. SET UP TOBY'S COMPUTER
26. FOG MASK OVER SHOWER

11:08:04
22:14
14:10
360

1
360
93
453

ADD MEAN WHITE TOURNAMENTS END

23ND JUNE

1. PUT NEW SCENES IN EDIT
2. ADD BUZZING NOISE TO CAMERA GIRL
3. SET UP KID ON YOUTUBE SCENE
4. ANIMATE CAM ON YT SCENE
5. ADD ARROW IN DADS HEAD
6. SET UP FATHER + SON PARK SCENE
7. MAKE SON DIFFERENT
8. RENDER CAT FENCE
9. RENDER CAM GIRL CRYING
10. ADD BIZARRE C TO CAM GIRL
11. DELAY VOCALS ON ATTIC LOVEBIRDS
12. RENDER PHARMACY
13. COMP HAPPY GUY GHOST

15. FIX PIANO SEQ + RENDER + ADD ROTATING CAMERA
16. ORDER TOBYS COMPUTER
17. COMP PHARMACIST
18. ADD BLOWY TOY ACT FOR DICK EAR
19. SET UP FATHER IN HOSPITAL SCENE
20. SET UP AUDIENCE FILE
21. PIANO AE FIX TIMING
22. EXPORT NEW AUDIO FR SIM
23. RENDER EXTENDED CLOUDS EARTH THE END 5

24. PREPARE VOCALS FOR KIRSTEN! AE
25. GHOST HAND AE
26. ADD FRAME AROUND OLD FOLKS FRAME

20TH JUNE

1. ADD BUZZING NOISE TO CAM GIRL
2. OLD FOLKS HM. EXTEND SLOW WALK
3. LR ADD CIRCS COLOUR CARD ARRIVAL

URGENT BG CHARS
FIREMEN.
TRAIN

FIX SITCOM TIMING

6x9

58   57
37   37
95   94

75   37/25
5
62   62
25   25
62
62-25   37

17 JUNE / 18 JUNE

1. REVISE AUDIO, EXAMINE LEVELS ON ALL CLIPS
2. INSERT RUFF ENVIRON MENTS
3. EXTEND COW SCENE + INCLUDE TEXT
4. ADD BLOOD TO TRAIN SEQ +
5. ADD TRANSITION TO TRAIN SEQ TOO
6. ADD FLOATING PARTICLE TO RABBIT HEAD
7. ADD APPLAUSE LIGHT AT RIGHT TIMES
8. RE SEQUENCE OLD FOLKS BIT, ADD SMALL MIKE
9. RETIME SHIT SEQ AND MOVE MOUTHS MORE
10. PRE INTERMISSION → HAVE CLOCKWIND + CIRCLE APPEAR + TEXT ARRIVE → QUICK QUICK

27TH JUNE
1. HALF SPEED ON 22?
2. TAXI DRIVE AWAY SFX
3. SLOWER FADE ON PACIFIER
4. SAD MUSIC OVER GIRL CRYING
5. GET MUSIC OVER L22
6. TILD ~~SOUNDS~~ TO SEATING
7. BLOOD CREEPING HORIZONTALLY
8. MICROWAVE ON SFX
9. SET UP TEACHER SCENES
10. CHAIR ROLLING SFX HAPPY GUY OLD FOLKS
11. MAKE ROOM EXTREMELY LONG FATHER & SON
12. PATERNAL AFFECTION "EPISODE 12"

"FRISBEE OF MISGUIDED PATERNAL ADVICE" SOME GIFTS

KEY TRAMP ADVENTURE

28th JUNE
1. PACK FOR PARIS
2. ~~~~
3. MAKE DVD WITH VIDEO
4. WRITE LETTER TO SERGIO
5. PRINT & PREPARE LETTER
6. HEAD TO POST OFFICE
7. SHIP 35 MM REEL MAKE GIFTS
8. BRING BUS. CARDS
9. ADD PRESS FELT TO WEBSITE
10. SHIP DUDES DVDS/SKS
11. RBILL

THE EXTERNAL WORLD

1 JULY
1. FIGURE OUT BUG CRAWLING PARTS
2. ADD/INSTANCE BUGS
3. RENDER TEACHER BUGS
4. ANIMATE HITLER RUN SCN
5. ANIMATE TEACHER CAMERA
6. LOOK AT OLD FOLKS SCENE
7. EXTEND CORRIDOR SCENE
8. FIX FELIX SHAPE
9. MOVE WHEEL CHAIR OLD DUDE. TO MIDDLE
10. ADD IN PROPER NEW TRAIN CHARS.
11. RENDER & COMPOSE TEACHER.
12. ADD TEACHER SCN TO EDIT
13. THINK ABOUT TITLE DESIGN. DO STH BASIC
14. RENDER NEW TITLE BITS
15. OLD FOLKS FOR 2S ON AE.

4 JULY
1. COMPLETE ALL 4 DAY TASKS
2. CALL JON/ITALIC TO V
3. CHECK TRAMP SCENE
4. INSTALL NEW SCRIPTS
5. GET TEACHER TO FOLD ARMS.
6. CONVERT TEACHER TO 2S + FIX UP
7. ADD FELIX PAPER TO CORRIDOR, FIX
8. MAKE LIVE BURN THROUGH CHARACTER
9. MAKE ZOOM OUT FROM PAPER CITY
10. FIX FELIX EAT
11. MAKE OLD FOLKS STUFF TO 2S.
12. ADD "ACME" TEXT TO BORDER
13. ADD "LATER/MEANWHILE" OLD TITLE CARD FOR START OF SITTDOWN SCENE

22ND JUNE
1. CUT NEW SCENES IN EDIT
2. ADD BUZZING NOISE TO CAMERA GIRL
3. SET UP KID ON YOUTUBE SCENE
4. ANIMATE CAM ON YT SCENE
5. ADD ACTION IN DADS HEAD
6. SET UP FATHER & SON PARK SCENE
7. MAKE SON DIFFERENT
8. RENDER CAT PETTING
9. RENDER CAM GIRL CRYING
10. ADD BIZARRE C TO CAM GIRL
11. DELAY MOSAIC ON RICE LOVEBIRDS
12. RENDER PHARMACY
13. COMP HAPPY GUY + GHOST

14. FIX PIANO SEQ + RENDER + ADD ROTATING CAMERA
15. BORDER TOBYS COMPUTER
16. COMP PHARMACIST
17. ADD BLOW'Y TOY FCT FOR DICK FOR
18. SET UP FATHER IN HOSPITAL SCENE
19. SET UP AUDIENCE FILE
20. PIANO AE FIX
21. EXPORT NEW AUDIO RE SIM.
22. RENDER EXTENDED CLOUDS + EARTH WITH DVD
23. PREPARE VOCALS FOR KIRSTEN!
24. GHOST TRAIN
AE
25. ADD FRAME AROUND OLD FOLKS FRAME

20TH JUNE
1. ADD BUZZING NOISE TO CAM GIRL
2. OLD FOLKS HM. EXTEND SLOW WALK.
3. LB ADD CIRCS. COLOUR CARD ARRIVAL
URGENT BG CHARS
FIREMEN.
TRAIN
FIX SITCOM TIMING

6x9
58   57
37   37
95   94
        37
    75   25
     5
     62
62   25
        37
62-25

17 JUNE / 18 JUNE
1. REVISE AUDIO, EXAMINE LEVELS ON ALL CLIPS
3. INSERT RUFF ENVIRON-MENTS
4. EXTEND COW SCENE. INCLUDE TEXT
5. ADD BLOOD TO TRAIN SEQ +
6. ADD TRANSITION TO TRAIN SEQ TOO
7. ADD FLOATING PARTICLES TO RABBIT HEAD
8. ADD APPLAUSE LIGHT AT RIGHT TIMES
9. RE SEQUENCE OLD FOLKS BIT, ADD SMALL MILE
10. RETIME SHIT SEQ AND MOVE MOUTHS MORE
11. PRE INTERMISSION D HAVE CLOCK WIND + CIRCLE APPEAR + TEXT ARRIVE
QUICK QUICK

OSBERT PARKER

"I may or may not have an idea in mind when I start work in my sketchbook, but whatever it is I'm developing, whether it's a technique, a character, a story, or simply an idea, my objective always remains the same—to playfully explore and to discover the unexpected."

Osbert Parker left Middlesex Polytechnic in 1988 with a BA Honours in Graphic Design. Four years earlier he had gained a Diploma from Berkshire College of Art and Design. His graduation film *Clothes* (1988) gave him his first of three BAFTA nominations. The first two films in his "Noir" trilogy, *Film Noir* (2006) and *Yours Truly* (2007),

have been internationally acclaimed, winning awards at countless festivals including nominations for the Short Animation BAFTA and the Palme d'Or at the Cannes International Film Festival. As well as being a successful filmmaker, he is also a freelance commercials director: his commercial credits include clients such as Coca-Cola, Nike, Budweiser, Gatorade, the World Wildlife Fund, and MTV. He lives in London, but works all around the world and is currently creating the third "Noir" short, developing a mixed-media feature and directing a series of eight short films for BAFTA winning show, *Misfits*, on Channel 4 in the UK.

OPPOSITE *"I purchased a bunch of fantastic 1950s movie lobby cards in Cuba, used here in part with an image from a 1937–38 furnishing catalogue purchased in a Los Angeles thrift store some years earlier. This collage was inspired by the catalogue title page, which in turn directly inspired a scene in my shorts,* Film Noir, *and a plot point in* Yours Truly.*"*

ABOVE Film still from *Yours Truly*, 2007

"I find that working spontaneously, for example, sketching, cutting out, and creating collages are some excellent and immediate ways of creating that unexpected happening or interesting juxtapositions."

"The sketchbook is my playground. It's a world where there are absolutely no agencies, no clients, no budgets, and no rules."

ABOVE *"A collage of colour and B&W photocopies, masking tape, graphite, metal pins and thread make up an underworld character as inspiration for my noir shorts. The tangible and physical reality of characters are important to me and I try to get below their skin and communicate this through the way I choose to use material and motion."*

OPPOSITE *"Pen and ink drawing with photo cut-out and Tipp-Ex was another image created in my sketchbook as part of a series of animated ideas, entitled 'Theatre of Nonsense' through play. This specific image was later used as reference for another underworld character made from collage in my noir shorts."*

"The pages within my sketchbooks are an exploratory and personal visual record of my pursuit of a unique cinematic language which comes not only from my mind, but also from my heart, with passion." [1]

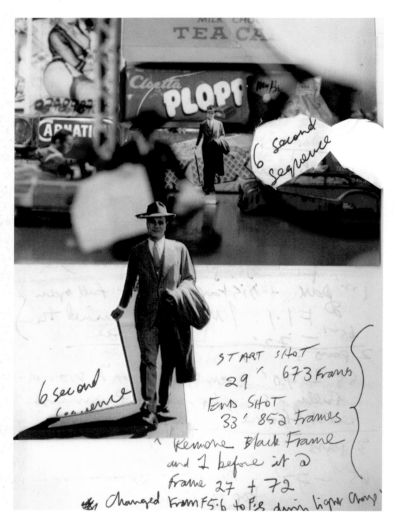

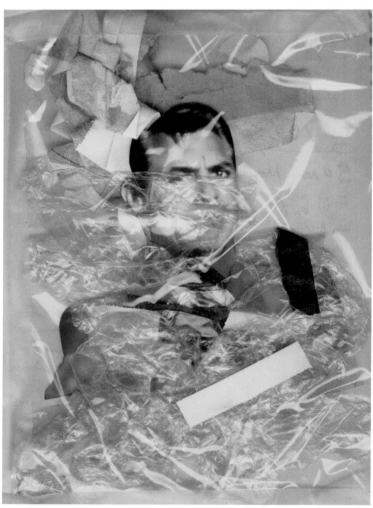

ABOVE LEFT *"This image is taken from my camera notebook, detailing my camera set-ups (length of shot in frames, f-stop and any mistakes) during animation tests and production shots. This is a 35 mm still of a 3D set with 2D photo cut-outs, toy cars, strange chocolate bars purchased in different European cities, and telephone calling cards, which made me think of what personal billboards of the future may look like."*

ABOVE RIGHT *"This is a production cut-out test still from* Film Noir. *It is used here in my sketchbook out of context as a photo-collage to suggest a different situation within entrapped plastic and masking tape. The highlights are picked up from the scanner and used directly as inspiration for a lighting set-up of a completely different scene within the same film."*

OPPOSITE Film stills from *Film Noir*, 2006

1 Passages quoted were originally published in *Communication Arts Magazine*, March/April 1996

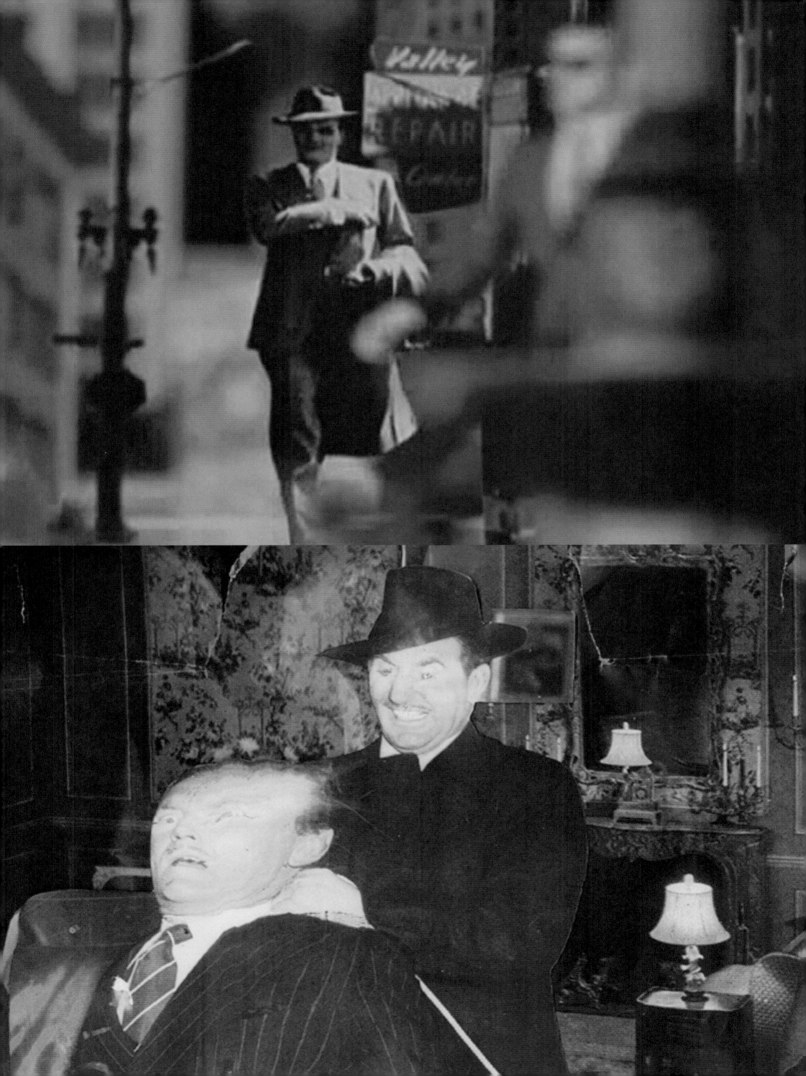

"There are basically two types of drawing. Let's describe one as real object—eye—brain—hand—result; and the second as brain—hand—result. When I draw, I follow the second progression. Consequently, my drawings don't directly reference a physical or real prototype. I draw with a specific objective in mind—or without one, as the case may be."

Priit Pärn was born in 1946 in Tallinn, Estonia. He earned a degree from the Department of Biology at the University of Tartu in 1970 and started working at the Tallinn Botanical Garden as a plant ecologist. Since 1976, he has worked as an art director and animated film director at the Joonisfilm, Tallinnfilm Studio and Eesti Joonisfilm Studio. His work has featured in over 30 exhibitions in various European countries and Canada and in 2007 he had a solo exhibition at the Kumu Art Museum in Estonia. From 1994 to 2007 Pärn was the artistic director of the animation department of the Turku School of Arts and Communication in Finland and in 2006 became the director of the animation department at the Estonian Academy of Arts. Pärn has written, directed, and designed 11 long-form animated films, as well as a host of short films and commercials. His films include *Breakfast on the Grass* (1987), *Hotel E* (1992), *1895* (co-directed with Janno Põldma, 1995), *Night of the Carrots* (1998), *Karl and Marilyn* (2003), *Life without Gabriella Ferri* (co-directed with Olga Pärn, 2008), and *Divers in the Rain* (co-directed with Olga Pärn, 2010). He has received five life-time achievement awards: from ASIFA, Fredrikstad, Krakow, Zagreb, and Cinema Jove film festivals. In 2008, he became a member of the European Film Academy.

ABOVE Film still from *Life without Gabriella Ferri*, 2008 OPPOSITE Sketches for *Life without Gabriella Ferri*, 2007

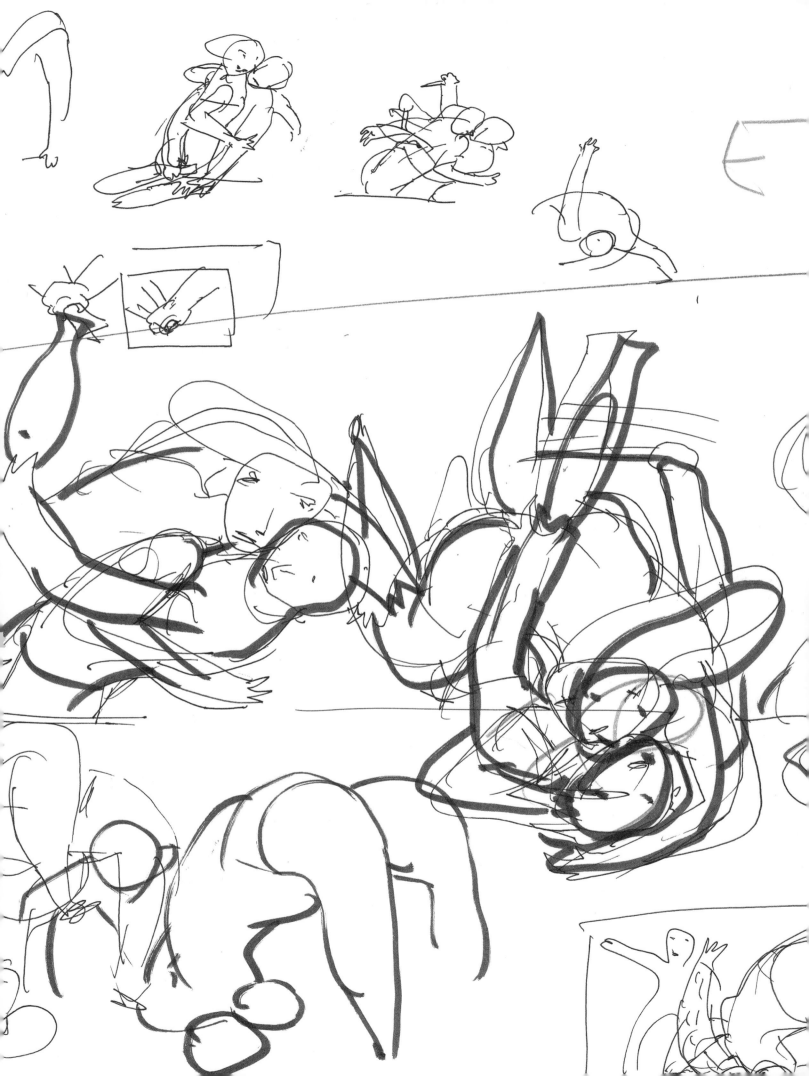

"When I draw, I need a table and loose sheets of paper—not paper bound together in a book. I almost never use an eraser. If I feel that something has to be fixed, I just throw the drawing away and make a new one. And it is always better than the previous one."

Sketches for *Karl and Marilyn*, 2002

"When one of my films is in production I have to draw thousands and thousands of images. Even though I create the characters and situations, my freedom is limited by the decisions I make before I start production. So, sometimes it's really refreshing to take a break from my own strict framework and to draw without limitations and without reason."

Sketches for *Karl and Marilyn*, 2002

"It is very important to me to draw without a specific goal in mind. It becomes about enjoying the line, playing with shapes and lines, creating images and destroying visual clichés."

Film still from *Life without Gabriella Ferri*, 2008

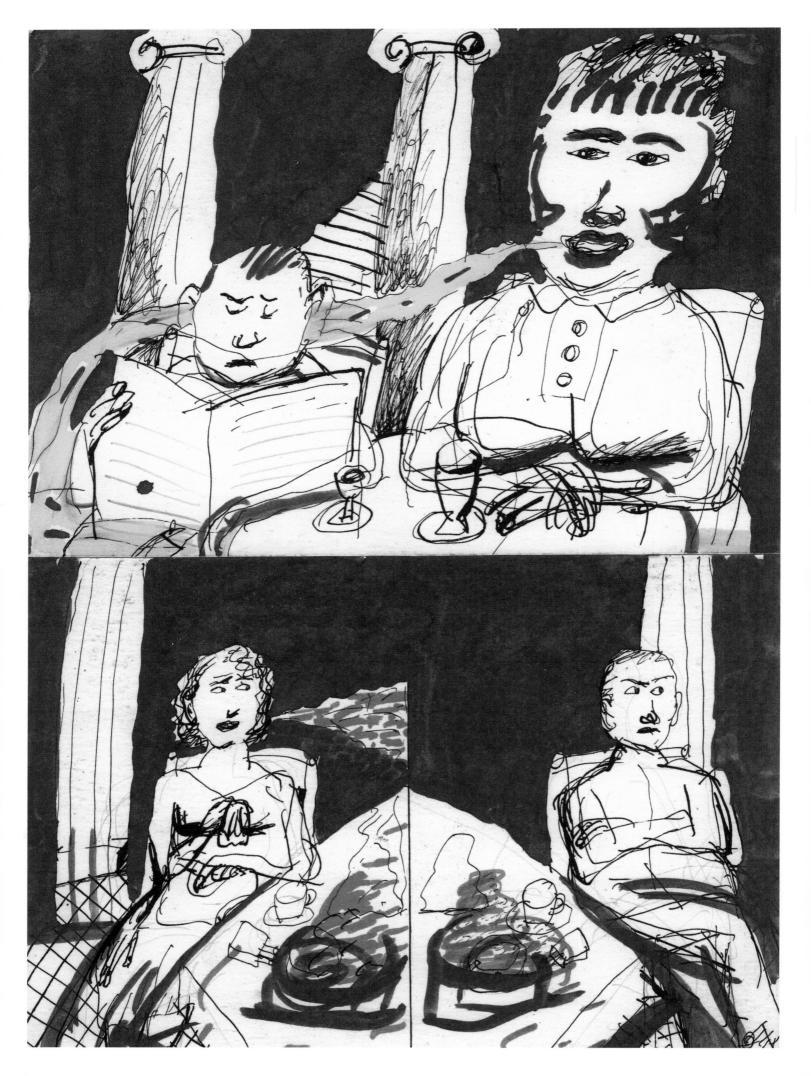

MICHAELA PAVLÁTOVÁ

"I always have to draw when I work on a film, simply because things can't always be articulated in words. Many ideas are indescribable and rely on graphics, shapes, pictures. I also draw to train my hand—for the same reason that you would practise the violin. If you draw electronically (at least in my experience), you don't feel the sensuousness of a pencil touching paper, and you lose your technique."

Michaela Pavlátová was born in 1961 in Prague, Czech Republic. She studied animation at VSUP Academy of Arts, Architecture and Design in Prague. As an animation film director, her films have received numerous awards at international film festivals, including an Oscar nomination for *Words, Words, Words* (1991), as well as the Grand Prix in Montreal, and accolades at Berlin, Tampere, Hiroshima, and Stuttgart. Her short animated film, *Répète* (1995), also won a series of awards, including the Grand Prix at the Hiroshima International Animation Festival and the Golden Bear in Berlin. In 2006 she made *The Carnival of the Animals* (2006), together with illustrator Vratislav Hlavaty, which won the Grand Prix in Espinho. Her most recent short animation film *Tram* (2011) won the Cristal Prize at Annecy. She also directed two live-action feature films, *Faithless Games* (2003) and *Night Owls* (2008). Pavlátová lives and works in Prague.

Sketches for the film *Words, Words, Words*

26

pondělí / monday

zora

27

úterý / tuesday

ingrid

28

středa / wednesday

otýlie

29

čtvrtek / thursday

zdislava

30

pátek / friday

robin

31

sobota / saturday

marika

01

neděle / sunday

hynek

23

pondělí / monday

yvona

24

úterý / tuesday

gabriel

25

středa / wednesday

marián

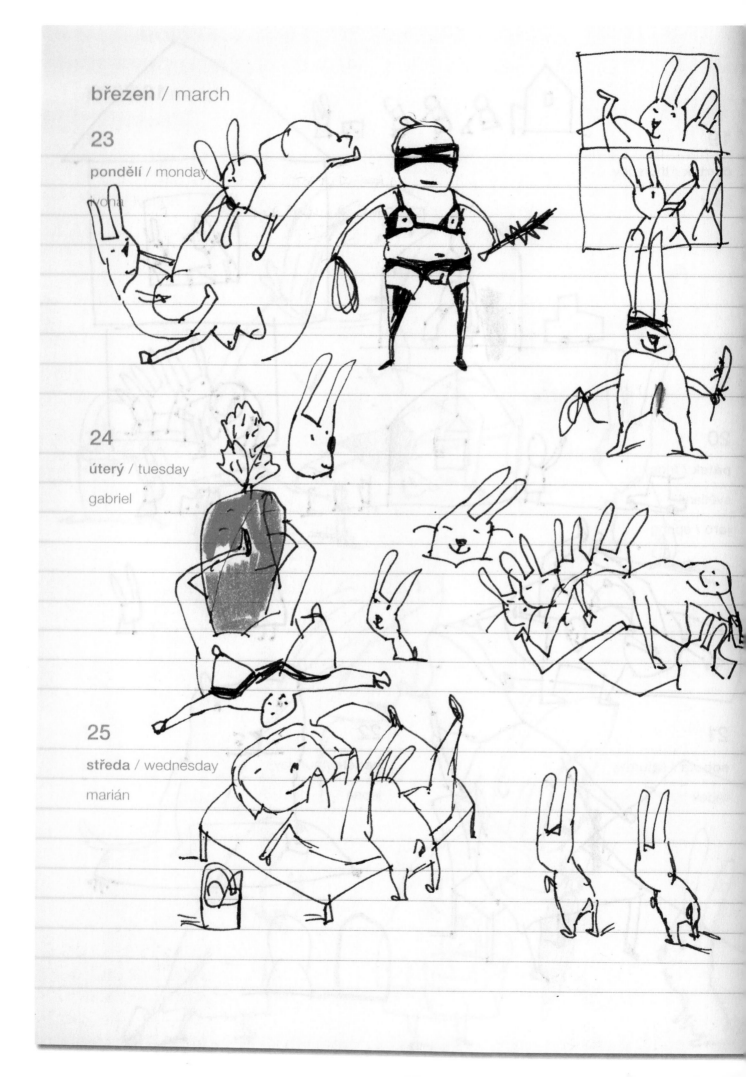

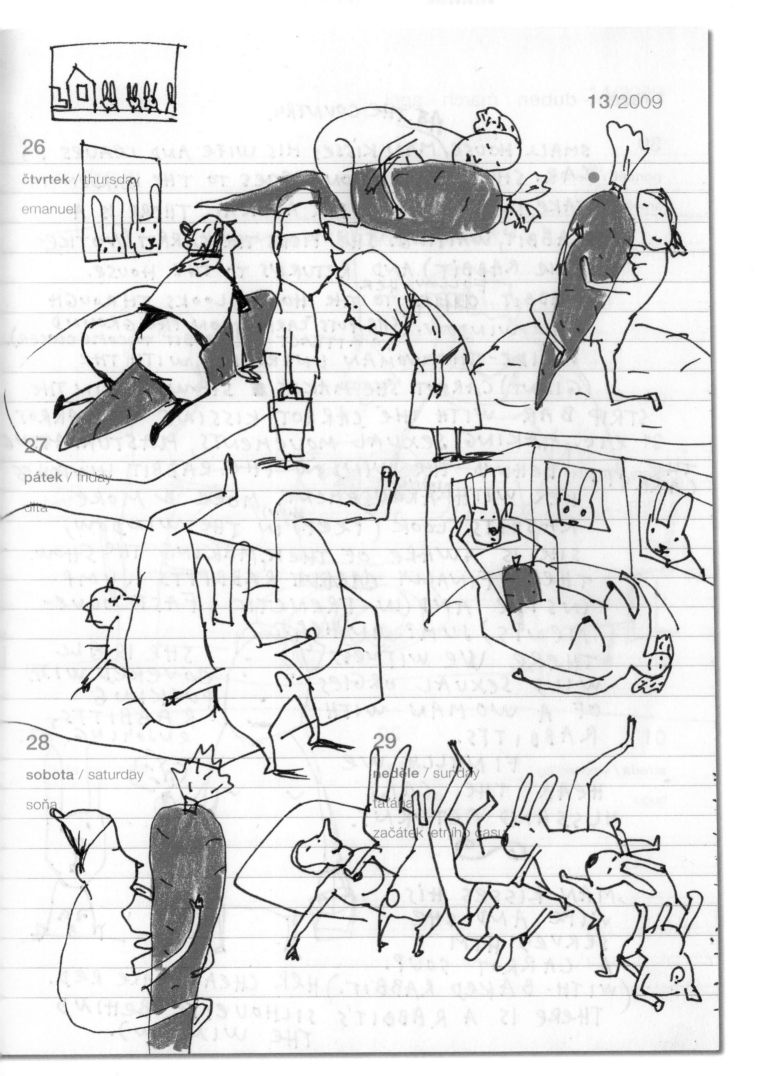

26
čtvrtek / thursday
emanuel

27
pátek / friday
dita

28
sobota / saturday
soňa

29
neděle / sunday
taťána
začátek letního času

5. ... a câmara acompanha a sombra do peixe que se trans-forma em tubarão, enquanto outros objectos passam em 1º plano também projectando sombras: telefone, caixa de lápis de

4. A sombra projectada do peixe "autonomiza-se"...

6. em sentido contrário surge uma nova luz que projecta a sombra de um dino-ssauro... (Gertie, Winsor McCay?)

7. a câmara continua e faz aumentar a sombra do dinossauro. O tubarão assusta-se e salta para trás

8. Em 1º plano aparece o cabo de uma colher que revela a origem da sombra...

9. ... que não passa afinal de uma formiguinha.

10. A luz acaba de passar e deixa-nos às escuras.

11. Uma nova luz revela-nos novos objectos. Distinguimos um garfo e a sua sombra projectada

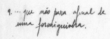

12. A sombra do garfo, trans-formada em mão de Nosferatu de Murnau, é projectada sobre o busto de um manequim ou escultu-ra.

13. Por sua vez a sombra do manequim, projectada na parede torna a forma de sombra de "Ivan, o Terrível"

14. A câmara continua a acompanhar o movimento de luz...

15. que projecta na parede sombras (abstractas) de objectos "normais",...

16. ... percebido pelas margens de uma árvore.

17. As folhas da árvore ganham vida e voam, como pássaros,...

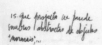

VII

18. e fica apenas um foco branco projectado na parede

19. Aparece a sombra de duas mãos que enquadram a imagem, como um rectângulo, à procura do seu enquadramento

20. Transfiguração do enquadramento final em "Combate da Odisseia nas Imagens"

REGINA PESSOA

"When I was a child, my uncle used to draw on the walls and doors of my grandmother's home with pieces of coal. Seeing him do this gave us a sense of freedom because we didn't have paper and pencils but we always had walls and doors. Maybe this stayed with me unconsciously because later...I made films using engraving techniques."

Regina Pessoa was born in Coimbra, Portugal, in 1969. She graduated from Oporto's School of Fine Arts in 1992 and started at Filmógrafo where she worked on the Abi Feijó animated films *The Outlaws* (1993), *Fado Lusitano* (1995), and *Stowaway* (2000). In 1999 she directed and animated her first independent film *The Night* using engraving on plaster plates. Her next film was *Tragic Story with Happy Ending* (2005) which has gone on to win more than 60 prizes around the world. Her most recent film is *Kali, The Little Vampire* (2012), an international co-production between Portugal, Canada, France, and Switzerland.

OPPOSITE Storyboards for the Odisseia nas Imagens festival, 2001
ABOVE Character sketch of Kali for the film *Kali, The Little Vampire*, 2012

"When the rush of work calms down, sometimes a spark or an idea comes into my head. It makes an impression on me and it's crucial I urgently write it down or make a rough drawing before it vanishes."

le début et la fin du temps
l'origine de toutes les formes
1
oiseau
cheval
les gens
la lune
et le soleil

Rarely do I dare to sketch in public. I never sketch in cafés or on the street: I'm always too ashamed of these instant drawings. So, I prefer to make them in the quiet of a dark corner, when nobody is watching. When I'm alone. Each time I open my sketchbooks, after a period of not using them, I'm surprised and amazed because the drawings seem so fresh and strong to me. So full of meaning. And then, I regret not sketching more often."

Film still from *Kali, The Little Vampire*, 2012

DAVID POLONSKY

"For some years now, I've been taking sketchbooks only on trips, usually to kill time on the planes and trains, and almost always to secretly draw portraits of other passengers. I found that I remember, even after years, every minute detail in the appearance and behaviour of the person that I drew in a travel sketchbook. Otherwise, my memory is somewhat foggy. It's like drawing puts you on a higher (or lower?) level of consciousness."

David Polonsky was born in Kiev, Russia, in 1973. In 1981 his family emigrated to Israel. In 1998 Polonsky graduated with honours from the Bezalel Academy of Arts and Design, Jerusalem. His illustrations appear in all the leading Israeli newspapers and magazines and his works in children's book illustration have won many awards. Polonsky was the art director and lead artist for the acclaimed film *Waltz with Bashir* (2008), directed by Ari Folman, which was nominated for an Academy Award and won the 2009 Golden Globe for Best Foreign Film. He is collaborating with Folman on a new feature film, *Congress*, to be released in 2013. He teaches illustration and animation at the Bezalel Academy of Arts and Design, Jerusalem and the Shenkar College of Engineering and Design, Tel Aviv.

Drawings made while travelling on trains

Sketches for *Waltz with Bashir*

ABOVE Sketches of dogs for *Waltz with Bashir*
OPPOSITE Film stills from *Waltz with Bashir*, 2008

JEFF SCHER

"I draw everywhere and anywhere between. I never set out to work in the notebook. It's more like the paperback that's hooked a reader. It appears in my hand whenever there's a 'down' time. Subways, late nights before bed, trains, boats, planes, waiting for my wife to finish online scrabble or my kid to make up his mind on his next move at chess. They are also notepads. Stray ideas I want to condemn to crayon. Phone numbers I'll be sure never to call. Things like that. It's where ideas come to stumble, crawl, and see if there're any takers. It's a place where my pen can dance with nobody watching. It's a place where I can pretend I'm Alexander Pope or Leonardo or Albrecht D. It's where my inner Timothy Leary can party. It's where the caveman within can come on out. It's like a party in a box. You open the box and it's instant party. You close the box and you're back here, which is nice too."

Jeff Scher, a painter and an experimental filmmaker, was born in Connecticut in 1954. His work is in the permanent collection of the Museum of Modern Art, New York, and has been screened at the Solomon R. Guggenheim Museum, New York, the Pompidou Centre in Paris, the San Francisco Museum of Modern Art, and at many film festivals around the world, including opening night at the New York Film Festival. Additionally, he has been commissioned to create work by HBO, HBO Family, PBS, IFC, the Sundance Channel, and more. Scher teaches graduate courses at the School of Visual Arts, New York and at NYU Tisch School of the Arts' Kanbar Institute of Film and Television's Animation program. A collection of his films, *Best of Times*, is available as a Vook on iTunes. His recent films include the signal film for the 50th Ann Arbor Film Festival, *September Mourning* (2011), and *Leaf or Death* (2012): both originally appeared in the *New York Times* online opinion page to which he frequently contributes essays and films. Additionally, he has made music videos for Bob Dylan, Paul Simon, and American Royalty. Scher currently lives in Brooklyn.

OPPOSITE *"Watercolor studies in preparation for the film Knock Knock, which became Bang-Bang and didn't look anything like these studies. These ideas turn up more in the much later music video Matchstick, for the band American Royalty."*

ABOVE Film still from *L'Eau Life*, 2007

"I really like the experimental part of experimental filmmaking. I've learned that the best way to have ideas is to just start making something. For me, it's like an antenna. As soon as I start working, drawing, pushing clay around... Almost instantly there's a little fish of an idea flopping on the floor, then another, then another. You have to pick a fish or they will keep dropping and flopping and you'd be up to your butt in flopping fish. Then when you've got your fish, you marry it. Then you go on a honeymoon. If you come back pregnant, you're in business. If not, you can try again or pick a new fish."

ABOVE, OPPOSITE, AND PAGES 210–11 *"This notebook was made around the time I acquired an Auricon 16 mm camera that could shoot bi-pack, or with two pieces of film in the gate at the same time. It was possible to shoot through travelling mattes in real time. These pages are mostly musings on how to exploit this odd technical opportunity for visual mischief. I was shooting through a lot of Moire type drawings, using positive and negative mattes in multiple passes."*

USE STROBE
W/ DIFF COLOUR
FILTERS

TRY RANDOM
FREQUENCIES

MYTHIC
STILL
LIFE

CYCLE A B C
R	Y	
B	Y	
B	Y	
R	Y	
R	Y	

COLORS
AGITATE

USE STROBE AS A WAY TO
MIX COLOR + ACTION ON
ALTERNATE FRAMES

OX VALANTINE NARROW
VARRIATIONS ON THEME

△ ○ △ ○ △

FLOWER - GO VARRIA...

WORDS IMITATION

GO STOP ∞

WATER

SUN SAND

33 SIDES OF MOIRÉ
PROJECTED ONTO
GEOMETRIC SHAPES
WHICH MOVE IN

BLACK VELVET

Project
Canvas

glow

color LANDSHAFT

triple exposed
panned L to R
over each
other

Square morphs to stay ahead
of each other A + B + C Y6 M

AURICON Bi-PACK
100' INT. + 100' MIXS

MATTE HAS ACTION

→ A SCENE
- SERIES
  OF scenes

Bi PACK

POSS + NEG

SCENE (A)

SCENE (B)

post NEG × 2

SCENE (C) ...

diff Between

AURICON → W/ 17:00 ft. MHG
PORTRAITS

RIPPLE MHG

A. MATTE
MOIRE

STREET
SCENE

RUN THROUGH
SEQUECE
OF STANV
STUFF

TWO dift TIMES

SAME
PLACE
SUPER

WACKY
MATTES

DOUBLE TIME

DIFF TIMES
ANV ACTION

SHOOT
MATTE HICON

NEG. OF STREET 2X

ALLISON SCHULNIK

"Everything has the capability of providing inspiration for me if I want: old books, movies, cartoons, flea markets, music, trash, food, dance, history, oceans, cake, black metal, musical theater, Dionne Warwick, etc. My brain blender takes these ingredients of earthly fact and blatant fiction and attempts to serve up a stage of tragedy, farce, and raw beauty. When I put something in material form, I hope to be capturing this other-world-buffoonery, or presenting a simple dignified moment."

Allison Schulnik, the daughter of an architect from the Bronx and a painter from British Columbia, received her BFA in Experimental Animation in 2000 from CalArts, Valencia, California. Her claymation videos include *Hobo Clown* (2008), *Forest* (2009), which was a commissioned music video for Brooklyn Band Grizzly Bear, and *Mound*

(2011). In addition to her award-winning films, Schulnik is also a recognized painter and sculptor. She has had solo exhibitions in Los Angeles, Chicago, New York, Montreal, Rome, and London, and has exhibited in both group shows and film screenings around the world at, for instance, the Garage Center for Contemporary Culture, Moscow; St. Louis Contemporary Art Museum; the Museum of Contemporary Art, Los Angeles; the Hammer Museum, Los Angeles; and the Hafia Museum of Art; and the Los Angeles County Museum of Art, among others. Her work can be seen in the public collections of the Nerman Museum of Contemporary Art Kansas; Museum of Contemporary Art San Diego; the Santa Barbara Museum of Art; Montreal Museum of Contemporary Art; Museé des Beaux Arts, Montreal; and the Laguna Art Museum, California. She lives and works in Los Angeles.

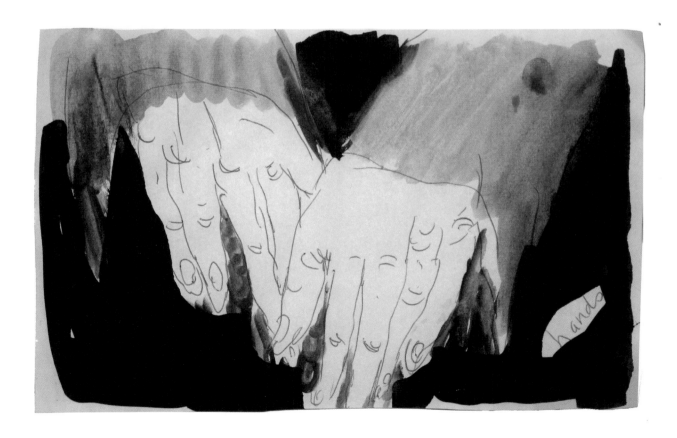

Early unused storyboards from *Mound*

TABLE—his view

old man looks down at creation

OLD Hobo stuff hangs Dollies trash etc...

pieces
Animal faces to gether
or skins to make MASK.

tools face

makes clown bearded mask— white (or black)
w/ animal skins, furs, old hobo
stuff, trash, etc...

or dumpster. then they are very small!

land and form black mare
of fear

then into gnome hollow... or to black
section?

Fear dancers (death) ← black hooded figures
women death angels
fly through sky.

come in through door
door already open

"Storyboards from Mound, some scenes were shot and others never made it into the film."

they take mask from him
and leave screen.

white haired old man, almost skeletal
walks into room
loving his cat.

* dead oct
hangs

← walks in, cat jumps down

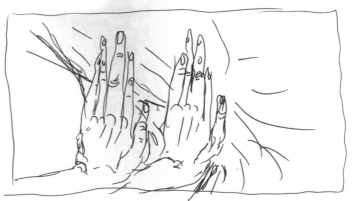

throbbing hole glower
insect enters it

pushing into another stomach

"My sketchbooks are essential to making work. They help flesh out ideas, keeping them as close to what's caged in my brain as possible."

"The fixation on the rejects, misfits, and their landscapes I depict is not intended to exploit deficiencies, but to find a valor in adversity."

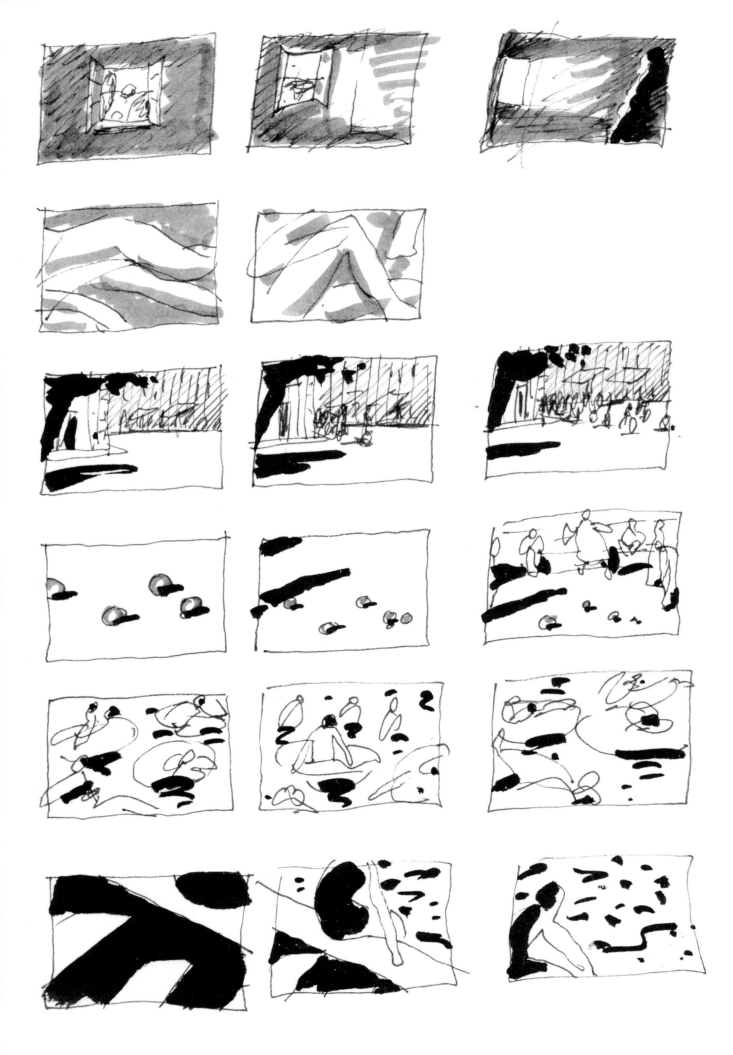

GEORGES SCHWIZGEBEL

"The animated films I love must put together characteristics of painting, music, and dance. Making a film alone lets me organize my time between creative and laborious work. Boring work becomes a break between creative works. Animation is an art of movement, with some constraints I appreciate. For example, the composition of the image changes constantly or the texture starts to vibrate because of the movement. By choice, I don't use dialogue. I am especially careful about the structure or composition of the film. Sometimes, music first gives me the subject of the film or the visual ideas, or maybe a story if I can tell it with images only. Being alone gives me the freedom to change the film when I'm doing it and to simplify: 'do the least and suggest more'. It is useful when we know how many drawings we need to make one animated film."

Georges Schwizgebel was born in Reconvilier, Switzerland, in 1944 and has created 16 short films that have received awards from Cannes, Annecy, Zagreb, Hiroshima, Stuttgart, Ottawa, and Espinho. Two of his films, *78 R.P.M.* (1985) and *The Ride to the Abyss* (1992), rank among the hundred most influential animated films on a list published by the Annecy International Animated Film Festival and the magazine *Variety* in 2006. *The Man without a Shadow* (*L'Homme sans ombre* 2004), Schwizgebel's first collaboration with the National Film Board of Canada, garnered 19 international awards. Although he first used the technique rotoscoping (*Perspectives*, 1975: *Off-side*, 1977), he later traded in this tool for a freer approach marked by the gestural application of color and the frequent use of geometric shapes in *Fugue* (1998), *The Young Girl and the Clouds* (2000), *JEU* (2006), *Retouches* (2008), and his most recent film *Romance* (2011).

MONTFLOUR   17.08.08

OPPOSITE Early research for the film *Romance* ABOVE Landscape sketch for the film *Romance*

FEVILLES MORTES A MONTFLOUR 7.7.05

"I like to elaborate a cycle, imagine movement in space and that follows the logic of a dream."

Film stills from *Romance*, 2011

M   H

"When I create a series of images I look to see how they contribute to what the story is that they are suggesting. Sometimes I realize there is a degree of sorrow attached to my images, especially when I pay attention to events that are taking place in the world. I can feel a sense of isolation in making art but then the work becomes part of a larger universe when it is finished and I don't forget that."

Maureen Selwood was born in Dublin, Ireland. She utilizes hand-drawn animation and live-action footage for films, installations, and performances. Selwood's process is often triggered by the role external devices, and their totemic value, play in our lives. In her most recent film, *A Modern Convenience* (2012), a machine becomes a substitute for intimacy against the backdrop of Niagara Falls. Among her other works are *Hail Mary* (1998) in which a centuries-old prayer morphs into a humorous black-and-white memoir. In *Mistaken Identity* (2001) Selwood creates an alluring deconstruction of the 1955 noir classic *Kiss Me Deadly*.

The expressively rendered *Drawing Lesson* (2006) sublimates a meditation on drawing and nature. While *I Started Early* (2007), based on a poem by Emily Dickinson, explores sexual awakening, *As You Desire Me* (2009), a single-channel version of an installation that was a reaction to the Iraq War, confronts sorrow and catastrophe. *How Much Better If Plymouth Rock Had Landed on the Pilgrims* (2012) conveys a hallucinogenic account of the Pilgrims' trip across the Atlantic. Many of her films have won international prizes, including *Odalisque* (1980), *The Rug* (1985), *This is Just to Say* (1987), *Pearls* (1988), and *Flying Circus: An Imagined Memoir* (1995) and have been screened at REDCAT, Los Angeles; Se-ma-for, Poland; Annecy International Animated Film Festival; Ottawa International Animation Festival; New York Film Festival; Stuttgart International Festival of Animated Film; Anima Mundi International Animation Festival of Brazil; Hong Kong International Film Festival; USA Film Festival; Ann Arbor Film Festival; Black Maria Film Festival; Northwest Film Center; Venice Biennale; Animac, Spain; and many others. Selwood has received grants from C.O.L.A. Individual Artist Fellowship, John Simon Guggenheim Memorial Foundation, New York State Council on the Arts, The Jerome Foundation, The American Film Institute, and a visiting artist residency at the MacDowell Colony, and Arteleku, Spain. She was the first animation artist to be awarded the Rome Prize from the American Academy in Rome. She is on the faculty of CalArts, Valencia, California and lives in Los Angeles.

OPPOSITE Drawing: A Shared Birthday ABOVE Film still from *As You Desire Me*, 2009

"I don't think one can escape a sense of self if a drawing is to be true."

Drawings for *A Modern Convenience*, 2012

"When I am drawing I feel that I am working deliberately towards something, even though I believe the unconscious has a role in how things come out."

ABOVE A sketchbook study for *Rules of the Universe*
OPPOSITE Film stills from *As You Desire Me*, 2009;
"Empire of Dreams" based on the poem by
Charles Simic

Shot/Board	Photoshop Element	Dialogue
19.12		

Animation Notes

Michael looks out
we see his pupils
momentarily
through
glasses.

Frame Motion

End Transition

cut

Immediately Dissolve to overhead
view of bed.

"He tested it on
himself"
(dissolve)

overhead view
w/ pattern
sheets.

"My sketchbooks have to be completely pressure free, no commitment, no responsibilities to anyone. Having multiple ones, or leaving them unfinished, or tearing pages out—these are ways to keep off the pressure to perform. Of course, when you think no one is looking, you do your better work, so then I end up showing it to people! Ha!"

Dash Shaw was born in Los Angeles in 1983. He started producing comics and zines while he was a BFA student at the School of Visual Arts. Since graduating, he has published several graphic novels: the telepathy comedy *Bodyworld* (2010) and the surreal family comedy *Bottomless Belly Button* (2008). His latest book is entitled *New School*. He was also the animator/director of IFC's *The Unclothed Man in the 35th Century AD* (2009) series and was the graphic artist for a comic art sequence in the film *Rabbit Hole* (2010). He has had solo exhibitions at the John Hope Franklin Center Gallery, curated by Diego Cortez, and at the Museum of Comic and Cartoon Art, New York. He is currently working on an animated feature. Shaw is based in Brooklyn.

"Storyboards for a feature film currently in progress—I draw the dissolves in the storyboards (opposite, below) so that I can make sure the dissolves are beautiful as they're happening. Since it's all drawn/controlled, unlike live-action films, you can do perfect dissolves, match-cuts, etc. It's a completely controlled cinema."

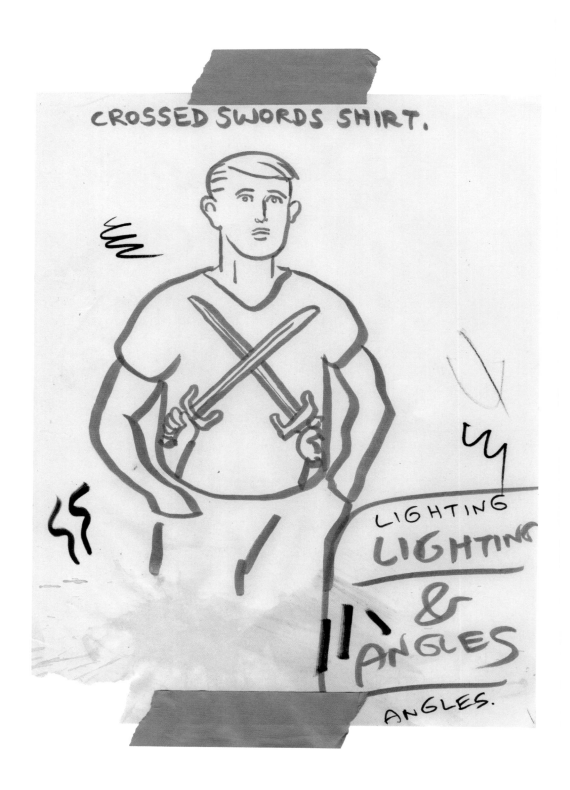

"These are two character costume sketches for a feature
film in progress which I have taped to my wall. The other
writing on it is scrap notes."

KNIGHT SHIRT

more
complicated,
for
still
scenes.

wig
shop!

Juliet
Mitchell's
The Sadian
WOMEN

"This is an early sketch of the layout of the Argus city in 'Shell,' which I later printed into a small zine on orange paper that I made about 100 copies of to give to people at a script reading for it."

235

DAVID SHRIGLEY

"I keep a notebook but not a sketchbook. When I keep a sketchbook, the work in it ends up being 'finished' work. I try not to draw things twice, though I guess this is pretty difficult in regards to animation. I'm a director rather than an animator, so I can get away without doing too many drawings. Things don't get better if they are re-drawn, in my experience. My notebook doesn't have many drawings in it. It mostly contains statements. I guess that's because I'm a sort of conceptual artist."

David Shrigley was born in Macclesfield, England, in 1968. After graduating from Glasgow School of Art in 1991, he has remained a firm fixture in Glasgow where he continues to live and work. Shrigley is an established artist, exhibiting widely in Europe and the US, including solo exhibitions at the Hayward Gallery, London; Yerba

Buena Center for the Arts, San Francisco; Turku Art Museum, Finland; Kelvingrove Art Gallery and Museum, Glasgow; M-Museum, Leuven, Belgium; Kunstmuseum, Lucerne, Switzerland; BALTIC Centre for Contemporary Art, Gateshead, UK; Hammer Museum, Los Angeles; and the CCS Museum at Bard College, Annandale-on-Hudson, New York, among others. He had his first major UK retrospective at the Hayward Gallery, London, in the spring of 2012. His animated work is a mixture of commercial films: *Good Song* (2003) with Shynola, and *Pringle of Scotland* (2010); and short films *Who I Am and What I Want* (2005) with Chris Shepherd, *The Door* (2007), *New Friends* (2009), and gallery specific pieces, including *The Flame* (2007), *Lightswitch* (2007), and *Sleep* (2008).

Sketchbook drawings and ideas for the film *New Friends*

"The notebook goes everywhere with me.
Losing it would be a terrible thing."

ABOVE Film still from *New Friends*, 2009
OPPOSITE Sketchbook storyboard for *New Friends*

MARCHING THE SOUND ↗ A MILITARY AND

ANCING TO JAMES BROWN'S FUNKY PEOPLE

Film stills from *New Friends*, 2009

CAT SOLEN

"I make my boards as detailed as possible... Money is always limited on every shoot, so anything that you can problem solve beforehand is beneficial. If I draw how I would like the lighting to look that makes it easier for my DP and producer to know which lights we need and don't need. I also try to get the depth of field and the camera angles as accurate as possible so that my team knows what kinds of lenses and grip equipment we need. This way we're not all guessing on set.

My storyboards, set, and puppet drawings help me answer the many questions people have. It's the best way to break down the project. I believe that if you can draw it, you can build it. It's my way of showing what I want the final product to be."

Cat Solen was born in Denver, Colorado, and grew up in Tucson, Arizona. She is a multimedia director who often combines live action, puppetry, and animation in her work. She has directed award-winning music videos for artists such as Bright Eyes, CSS, Sia, Deathcab for Cutie, Sean Lennon, and Local Natives. She has worked with actors Joseph Gordon-Levitt, Evan Rachel Wood, and Brady Corbet, as well as actor Terence Stamp and filmmakers Olivier and Michel Gondry. Her work consistently airs on Adult Swim and MTV. Last summer she was commissioned by Levi's to film an experimental collaboration with Swoon to promote the "Art in the Streets" show at MOCA Los Angeles. Solen currently lives and works in Los Angeles and is hard at work developing her first feature film.

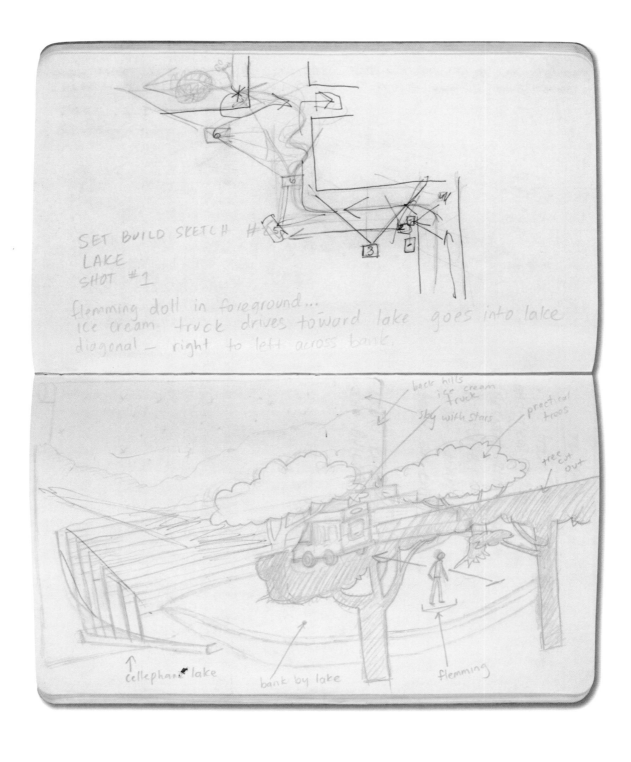

"When I'm making music videos with bands that I've never met before then drawing boards with them helps me get to know them better. Then on set, I already know their names and faces."

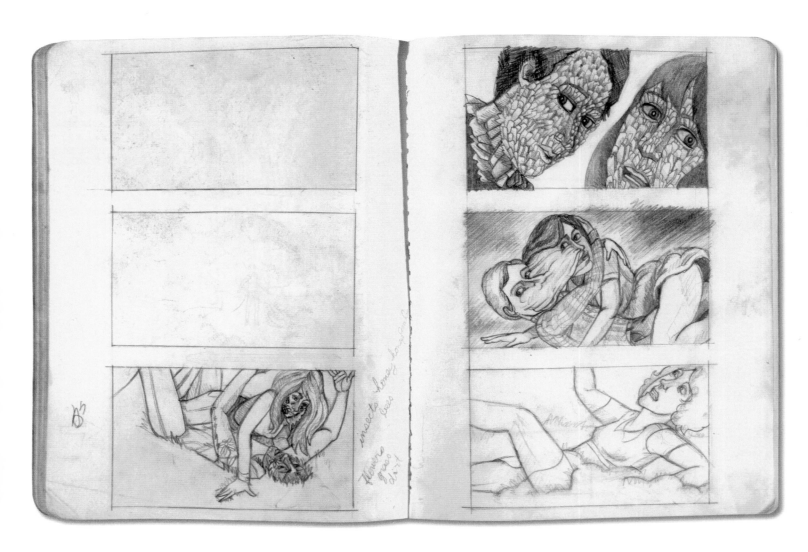

ABOVE Music video pitch

OPPOSITE Treatment boards

PAGES 246–47 A police car in *Backwash* spins out of control and hits a lamppost: the boards depict the specific moves that the car will make

PAGE 242 Movement map and set sketch for stop-motion miniature segments of *Backwash*, 2010, a web series for Sony/Crackle. The top drawing depicts a car chase and a crash map of how various sets will fit together in the edit. The bottom drawing is a map of the ice cream truck that drives into the lake.

PAGE 243 Work-in-progress comic book: character introduction

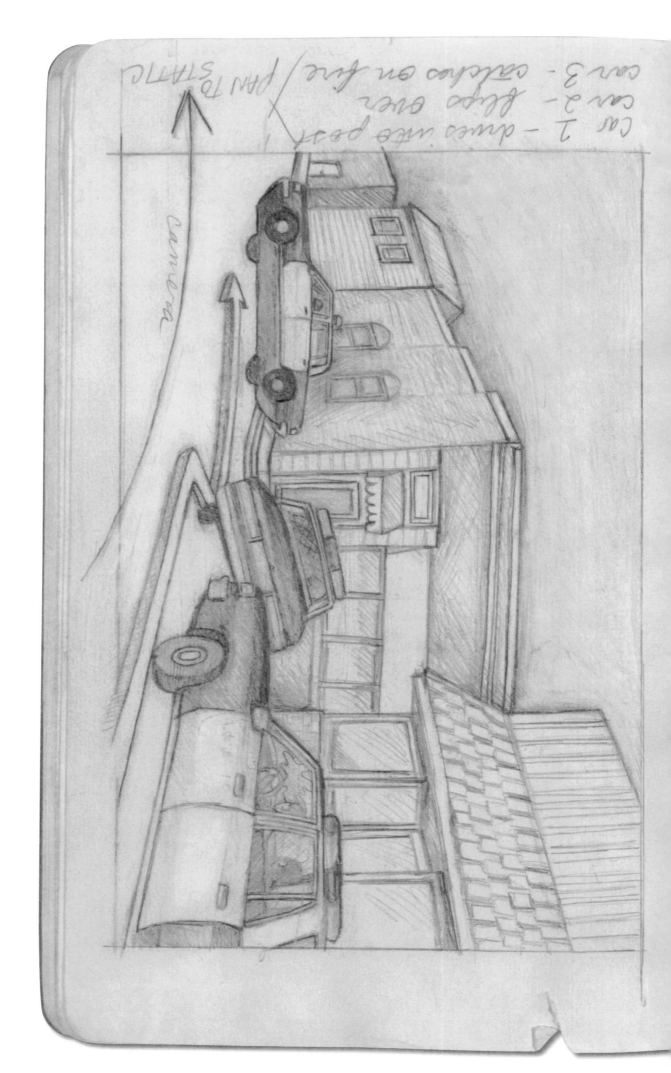

Car 1 - drive into post
Car 2 - flips over.
Car 3 - catches on fire / PAN TO START

camera

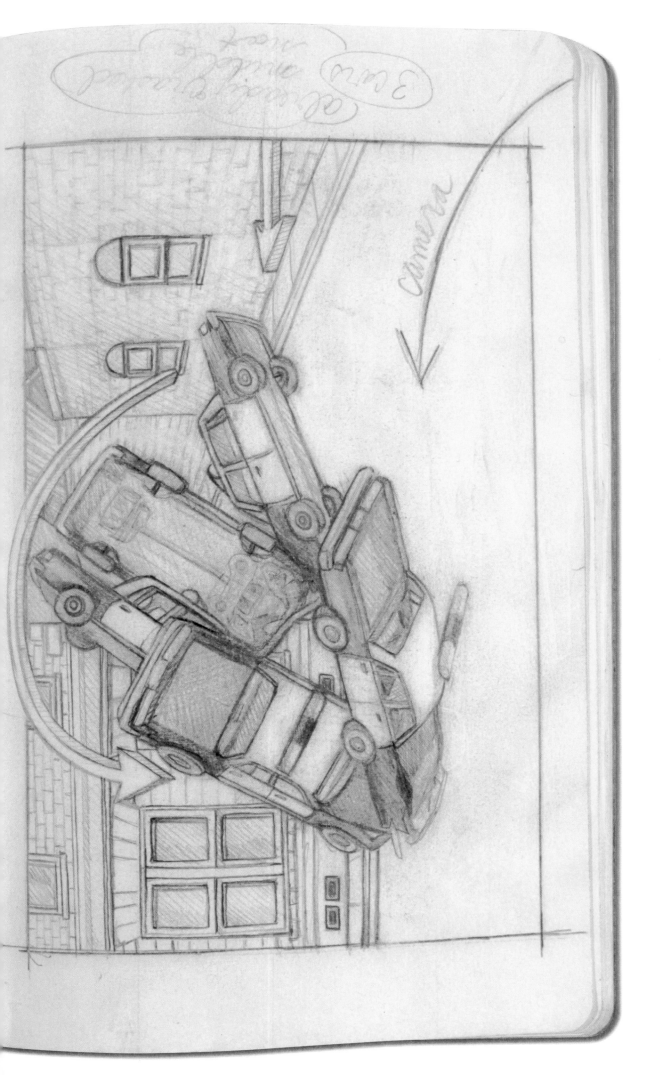

STACEY STEERS

"My ideas usually start out very simply, maybe as a single image. With Night Hunter *it was an image of a house with a woman, eggs, and snakes inside. I don't sketch really. I might write down an idea, but the real work starts with looking for images—in books and movies—that I think might relate to what I'm thinking about. I found a number of images for* Night Hunter *in the clipping room at the main library in New York City. I like to carry ideas around in my head and see if they seem to hold up. If I forget them, I assume they weren't right.*

I like to write out ideas as the construct starts to appear to me. I return to writing to try to clarify a film's structure, but almost all of my creative decisions are made in the process of working with my hands. I believe my particular collage technique of obsessively cutting and layering images, gluing one thing on top of another or cutting into an image and slipping something new behind it, mimics the way the mind processes experience and forms memories. Working this way triggers a particular type of reflection in me, and has taken my creative thinking into a more personal and deeper psychological terrain. Something I'm happy about."

Stacey Steers is an independent animation artist who lives and works in Boulder, Colorado. Her labour-intensive films are made up of thousands of individual handmade works on paper. Her animations include *The Black Sheep* (1986), *Watunna* (1990), *Totem* (1999), *Phantom Canyon* (2006), and *Night Hunter* (2011). They have screened at Sundance Film Festival, "New Directors New Films" at the Lincoln Center in New York, and numerous other festivals worldwide, winning national and international awards. Recently she has begun expanding her work to include installations that reflect on, and bring focus to, the films by placing production elements and/or film loops in a new context. Her work has been installed at the Corcoran Gallery, Washington, D.C., the Denver Art Museum, and the Hamburger Kunsthalle, Hamburg, among others. She has been the recipient of grants from the American Film Institute and Creative Capital, and has been an artist fellow at Harvard University, the MacDowell Colony, Ucross Foundation, the Liguria Study Center in Italy, and Yaddo, New York.

OPPOSITE Cut-out printed worms, snakes, and insects for *Night Hunter* ABOVE Film still from *Night Hunter*, 2011

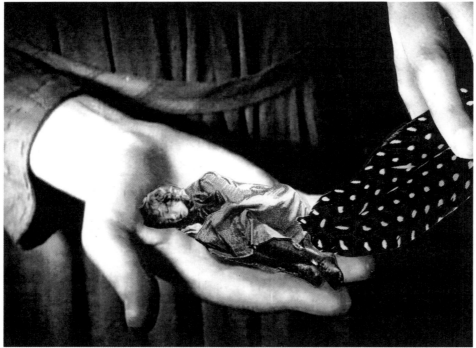

TOP Sketchbook collage color tests for *Night Hunter*
ABOVE Film still from *Night Hunter*, 2011
OPPOSITE Preliminary collage tests for *Night Hunter*

"I didn't used to work with collages. For years I drew animation, but it was always a struggle for me and I felt trapped by the particular expressive quality of my drawing style, so I looked for a new approach."

ABOVE Film stills from *Night Hunter*, 2011

OPPOSITE Cut-out printed grass and insects for *Night Hunter*

STEVEN SUBOTNICK

"I began exploring the idea intuitively through making images and animation sequences. Working in my sketchbook is a part of this process. I try to keep a sketchbook with me at all times because ideas can come at any moment: when I'm running an errand, while I'm working, when I'm about to go to sleep. For this reason, I like using a small sketchbook that easily fits in my pocket. I use the sketchbook as a way of recording my thoughts, or an image, or an influence of some kind. Occasionally, I use the sketchbook images just as they are. When I have enough artwork and animation made, I begin to edit. The process of editing is how I discover a meaningful structure in all my aesthetic responses. The entire process is one of discovery. I don't pre-plan the films. Rather, I uncover them through making them."

Steven Subotnick was born in San Francisco in 1956. He has been making independent films since 1985. He has worked as an animator, director, illustrator, author, and has taught animation at numerous institutions, including Rhode Island School of Design and Harvard University. His animated films are associative explorations of themes found in history, folklore, and nature, and include *Devil's Book* (1994), *Hairyman* (1998), *Glass Crow* (2004), *Jelly Fishers* (2009), *Boy* (2011), *Thine* (2011), *Two* (2011), *West* (2011), *Baby* (2012), and *Fight* (2012). He currently lives and works in Providence, Rhode Island.

Concept drawings for *Jelly Fishers*

Sketchbook drawings for the film *West* PAGES 258–59 Film stills from *Jelly Fishers*, 2009

Joanne Pell. Nose For beauty

CHRIS SULLIVAN

"I do not usually buy sketchbooks—I find them in the garbage. Abandoned sketchbooks, ledgers, and note pads are like aged wine, and often come with someone else's energy in them. One of my sketchbooks is the registry and by-laws of Kenmore Lodge no. 947 and has beautiful, brownish and aged lined paper."

Chris Sullivan is an animator, filmmaker, and performance artist whose experimental film and theater work spans 30 years. His work has been shown in festivals, theaters, and museums worldwide, including the World Festival of Animated Film, Zagreb; Ann Arbor Film Festival (winner of Best Animation award); New York City Short Film Festival;

Black Maria Film + Video Festival, New Jersey; Walker Art Center, Minneapolis; and Pacific Film Archive. Sullivan recently completed a feature-length animated film called *Consuming Spirits* for which he received Guggenheim and Rockefeller Media Arts Fellowships; it premiered at the Tribeca Film Festival, New York, in 2012. Since 2008 Sullivan has also created three evening-length performances, *The Outer Giants and their Moon, Aggression Therapy,* and *Mark the Encounter.* He is working on a new hand-drawn animated feature that has support from the Creative Capital Foundation. He lives and works in Chicago where he teaches at the School of the Art Institute of Chicago.

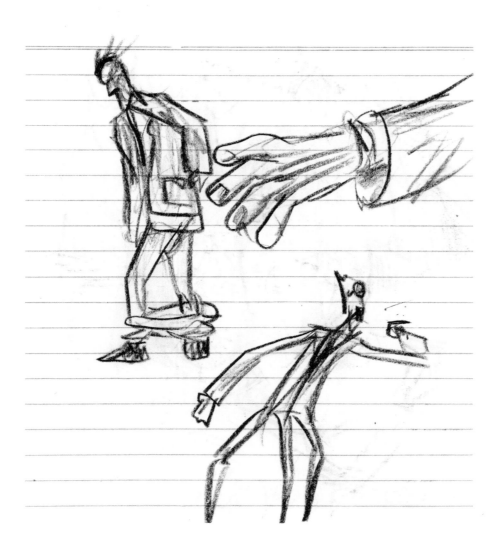

OPPOSITE, ABOVE, AND PAGES 262–63, 265 Drawings and ideas for *The Orbit of Minor Satellites* on notebook paper
PAGE 264 Film stills from *Consuming Spirits*, 2012

"I often will find the cure to my films, while drawing and writing, and put it down, like a discovery."

The ruins are alive not at find.

"*I use sketchbooks as a stream-of-conscience way to get to ideas. Very much like recalling a dream, I imagine where my film is, open my eyes, and see what is there.*"

MALCOLM SUTHERLAND

"I don't like to pencil things in first. I almost always draw with pen and ink, directly onto the paper. I think my need to draw comes from an addiction to the physical pleasure of drawing with ink on paper. For me, animation is a slightly different animal than drawing in a sketchbook— mainly because my focus is on movement instead of a single, detailed vision. I find the mark-making aspect of drawing remains the same for both, but with animation the single image becomes far less important than its relation to what comes before and after."

Malcolm Sutherland is originally from Calgary, Canada, and studied printmaking at the Alberta College of Art and Design. Arriving in Montreal in 2002, he started working at the National Film Board and then went on to study film at Concordia University. His short animated films,

including *Robot City* (2002), *Birdcalls* (2005), *The Tourists* (2007), *Forming Game* (2008), *Great Ambition* (2008), *Returning Round* (2008), *The Astronomer's Dream* (2009), *La Fête* (2010), *Light Forms* (2010), *Umbra* (2010), which was winner of the Vimeo 2012 Best Animation Award, and *Bout* (2011) have received awards and been screened at festivals worldwide. In addition to producing independent short films, he has worked in advertising, feature film, and television. His work has been showcased by McSweeney's, Animation World Network, Motionographer, *IdN* magazine, *Cartoon Brew*, Drawn, and on other major animation, illustration, and design sites from around the world. His comic book *Oola Dug* won the 2008 Expozine Alternative Press Award for Best Comic, and received a "Notable Book of 2008" distinction from "The Best American Comics," 2008. He currently lives in Montreal.

OPPOSITE AND ABOVE Sketchbook doodles PAGE 268, ABOVE "Space" studies BELOW *Birdcalls* drawings
PAGE 269, ABOVE Doodle and rhythm charts for *Forming Game* BELOW Composition thumbnail sketches

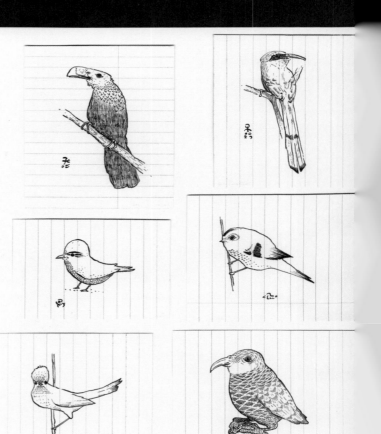

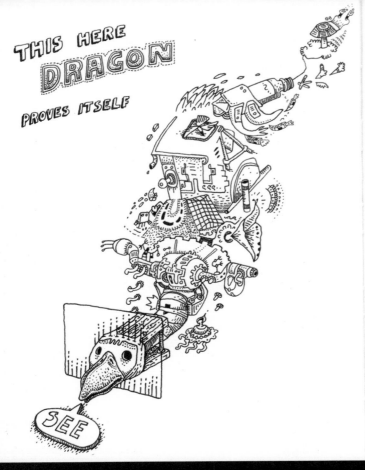

THIS HERE DRAGON

PROVES ITSELF

SEE

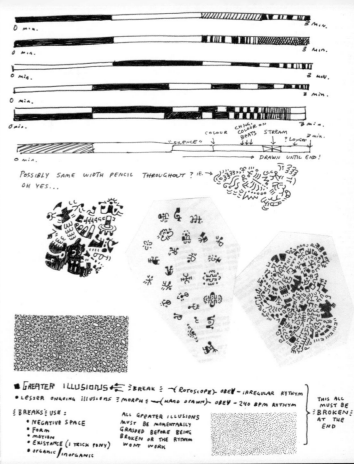

0 min. ... 3 min.

POSSIBLY SAME WIDTH PENCIL THROUGHOUT? IE. →
OH YES...

COLOUR CHANGE
COLOUR ON
BEATS STREAM
"SILENCE" LONGER
→ DRAWN UNTIL END!

■ GREATER ILLUSIONS ⇐ BREAK ⇒ (ROTOSCOPE) OBEY - IRREGULAR RYTHM
• LESSER ONGOING ILLUSIONS MORPH ⇒ (HAND DRAWN) OBEY - 240 BPM RYTHM

THIS ALL MUST BE BROKEN AT THE END

BREAKS USE:
• NEGATIVE SPACE
• FORM
• MOTION
• EXISTANCE (1 TRICK PONY)
• ORGANIC/INORGANIC

ALL GREATER ILLUSIONS MUST BE MOMENTARILY GRASPED BEFORE BEING BROKEN OR THE RYTHM WONT WORK

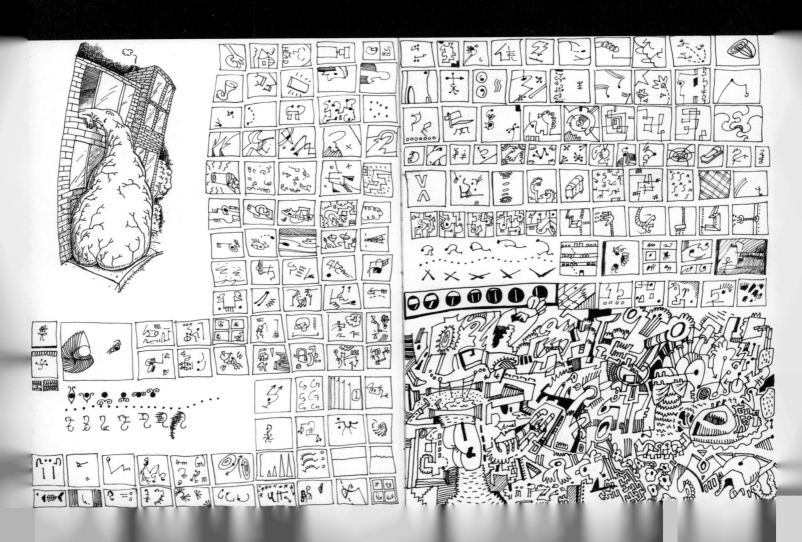

"I feel like most of my drawings were not made by me, that I just happened to be around when they were born…"

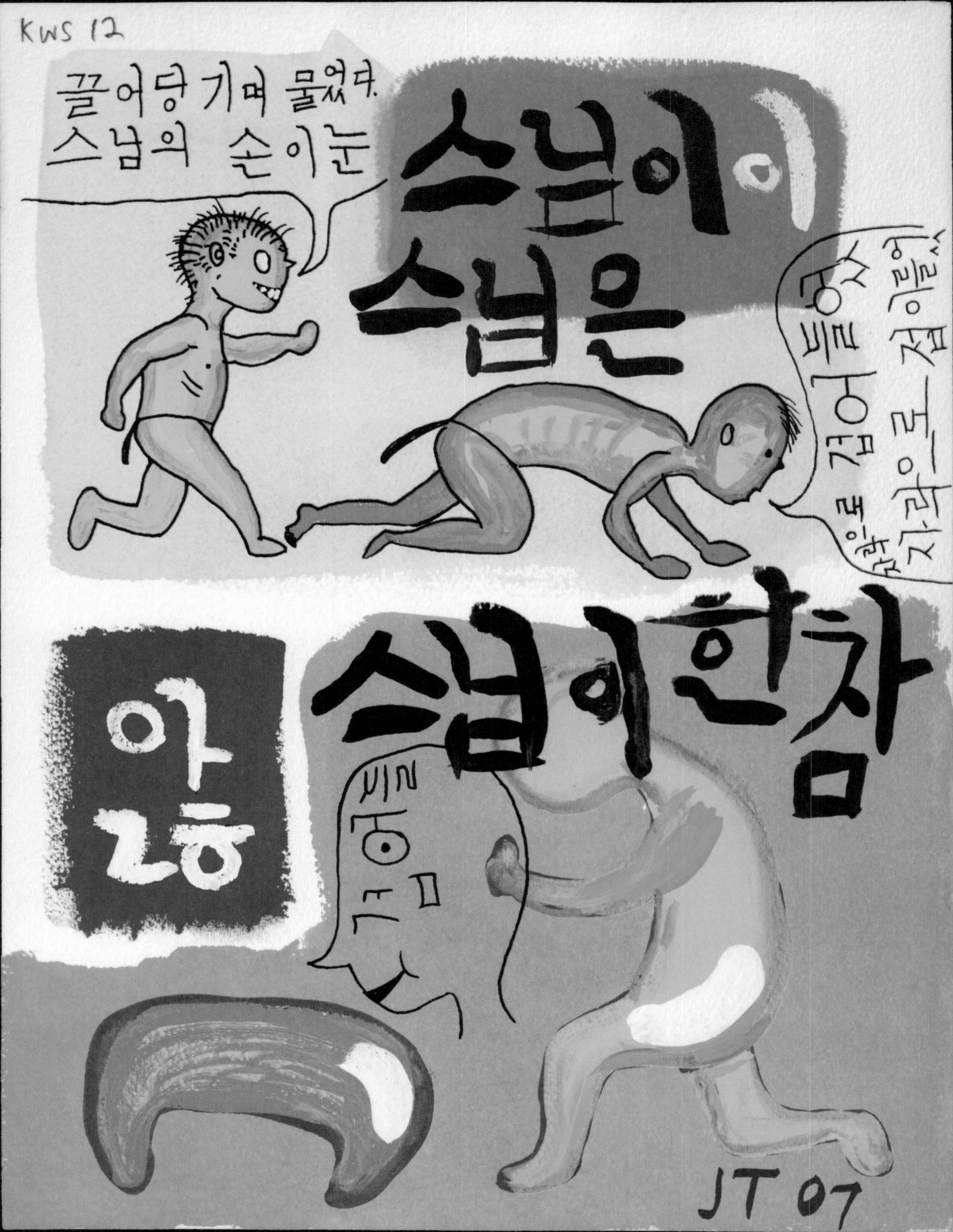

JIM TRAINOR

"Most of my drawing goes into animation. Occasionally, I have a burst of energy where I make a lot of sketches on a related idea. The sketchbook I call 'KWS' consists of gouache paintings of various images, onto which I copied random words from a Korean novel. I don't know Korean, but I am told that the random juxtaposition of images and words looks rather psychotic to a native speaker. It touches me somehow to know that these paintings have a level of meaning (or nonsense) that is unknown to their creator."

Jim Trainor was born in 1961 and grew up in Washington, D.C. He attended Columbia University in New York, graduating with a degree in English Literature in 1983. Among his films is a series of short animated films called *The Animals and their Limitations*, which includes *The Bats* (1998), *The Moschops* (2000), *The Magic Kingdom* (2003), and *Harmony* (2004). He is currently working on a new series of films, *Nascent Humanity*, which includes *The Presentation Theme* (2008). His work was shown at the 2004 Whitney Biennial and in 2010 he received the Alpert Award in the Arts. Trainor lives and works in Chicago, where he has been teaching at the School of the Art Institute of Chicago since 2000.

OPPOSITE Korean Word Salad #12, a sketchbook gouache painting ABOVE Film still from *The Presentation Theme*, 2008

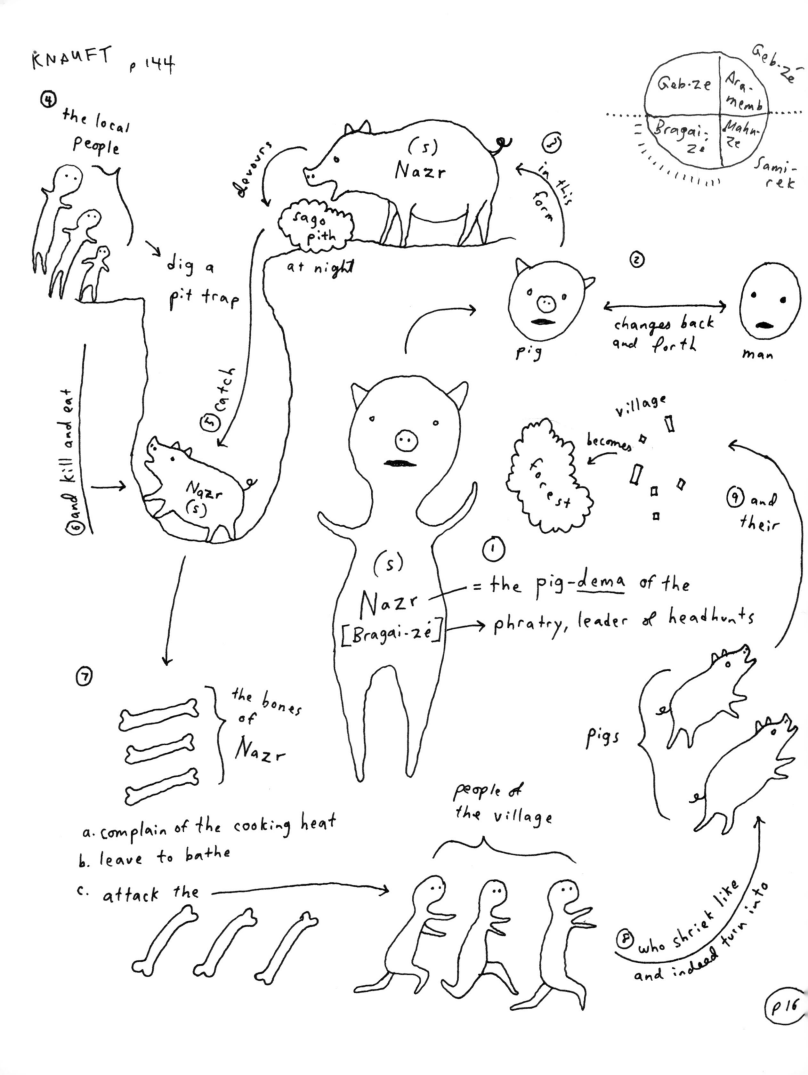

KNAUFT p 144

④ the local People

⑤ in this form

(s) Nazr

devours

sago pith at night

③ dig a pit trap

④ catch

⑥ and kill and eat

Nazr (s)

Geb·ze | Ara-memb
Bragai-ze | Mahn-ze
Geb·ze
Sami-rek

② changes back and forth

pig   man

village
becomes
forest

(s) Nazr [Bragai-zé] = the pig-dema of the phratry, leader of headhunts

⑨ and their

Pigs

⑦ the bones of Nazr

a. complain of the cooking heat
b. leave to bathe
c. attack the

people of the village

⑧ who shriek like and indeed turn into

p 16

"It's a pitfall of animation that the storyboards are often the true creative effort, while the animation itself becomes a sort of mechanical labour. I prefer to keep things looser in the drawing stage, then tighten it up in the editing."

"As for animation drawing, I never do conventional storyboarding to work up my ideas. Instead, I draw lots of random pictures on a related subject, then sort through them and arrange them in some kind of narrative order. Then I use each of the selected drawings as the starting point for a single shot. I animate forwards and backwards. Eventually a sequence emerges, which I then take to the animation stand. When I screen the footage, I look for gaps in narrative sense, which I then go back and fill in. This technique is not exactly economical, but it keeps me engaged with the process."

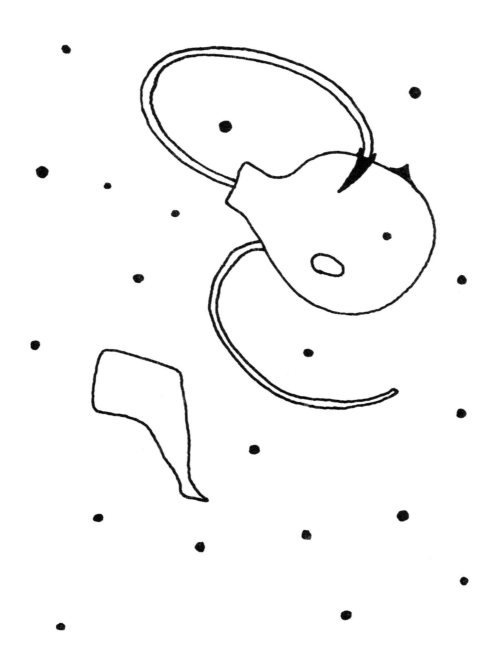

ABOVE Film still from *The Presentation Theme*, 2008
OPPOSITE Sketchbook notes for the *Nascent Humanity* series

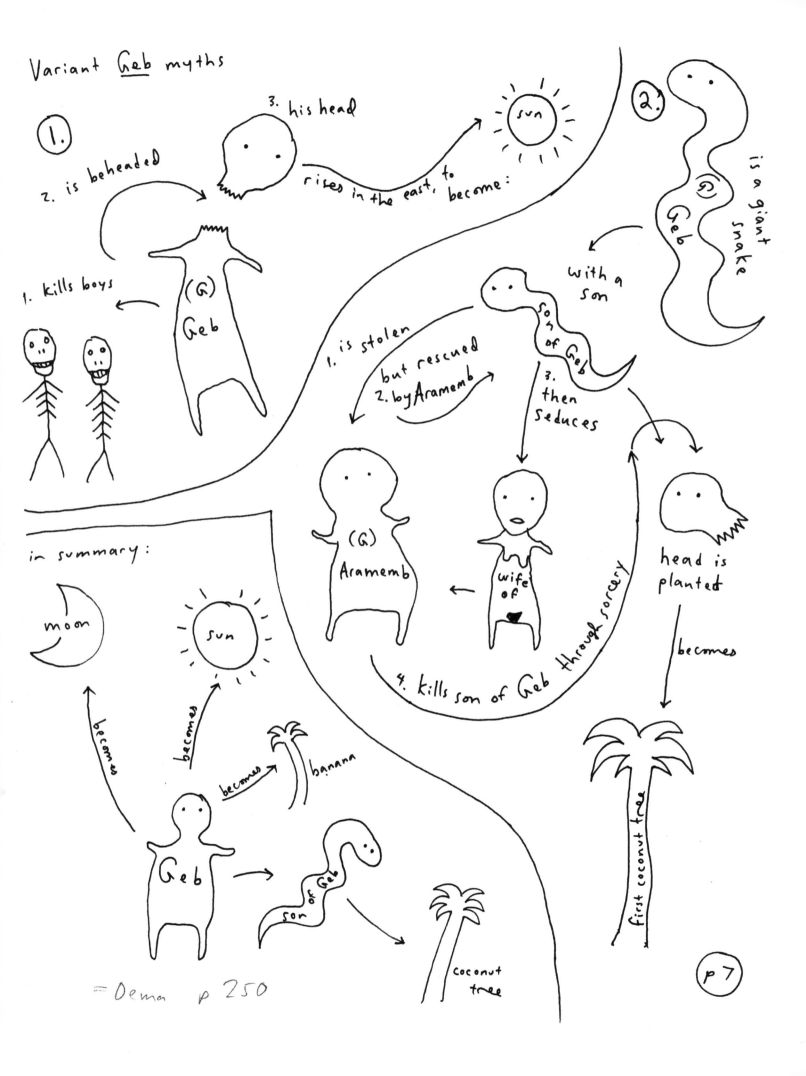

Variant Geb myths

1.

2. is beheaded

3. his head

rises in the east, to become:

sun

(G) Geb

1. kills boys

2.

is a giant snake

(G) Geb

with a son

son of Geb

1. is stolen

but rescued
2. by Aramemb

3. then seduces

(G) Aramemb

wife of

4. kills son of Geb through sorcery

head is planted

becomes

in summary:

moon

sun

becomes

becomes

becomes

banana

Geb

becomes

son of Geb

coconut tree

first coconut tree

= Dema p 250

p 7

REE TREWEEK

"I'll look at it and wonder who or what has appeared on the paper. I'll then wonder where they came from, what they like to eat, who they're friends with, what they hate. What is their relationship with other characters in the book? This is how their stories or ideas are brought to life. My sketchbooks act as a doorway to a world that would otherwise be hidden from me."

Ree Treweek forms a third of the fantasy art collective, The Black Heart Gang, whose focus largely concerns explorations into a realm best knows as "The Household," a universe that exists just beneath our Earth's crust and is powered by human bath water. Treweek grew up believing that a giant snake lived beneath her bathtub. He would drink up all her soapy bathwater and if she didn't jump out of the bath quickly enough the snake would swallow her too. She owes a lot to this terrifying reptile as it gave her cause to believe that other worlds exist all around us, yet somehow remain hidden from our eyes. The Gang have been exploring this realm since 2006, documenting its stories and inhabitants through sculpture, short films, books, and paintings. Treweek is also co-founder of the Gang's commercial counterpart Shy the Sun where she acts as Art Director, character designer, and concept developer. Shy the Sun has worked for clients such as United Airlines, American McGee's "Alice" game trailer as well as "The Beatles Rock Band" game in which Treweek designed the characters. The Black Heart Gang's first personal project *The Tale of How* (2006), featuring Treweek's darkly surreal illustrations, brought international acclaim. Treweek currently lives in Cape Town.

"I like people to look through my book, especially the people I work with. They often have ideas that I would have myself."

OPPOSITE Bear home ABOVE Lemon moles: Burpie and the Advisor

"I draw everywhere and anywhere. Currently, I have three big sketchbooks with leather-bound covers and old paper inside. They smell good when you open them. My ideas come as soon as the ink begins flowing on paper. Usually I have no idea what I'm going to start with. The ideas often come after the drawing happens."

ABOVE Wise men
OPPOSITE Film stills from *The Tale of How*, 2006
PAGES 284–85 The mole tribal village: Ree and Nyoman Kenyak

PAUL VESTER

"I work on a lightbox, in pencil, usually on any piece of paper that comes to hand. I also keep sketchbooks. Mainly these days I write in the sketchbooks, which are quite personal. Sometimes I stick a drawing in the sketchbook if I remember. I used to like drawing directly on cel with a brush, a long-haired sable, and black cel-vinyl ink (ink, not paint), which goes on very smoothly, dries fast, and is easy to scrape back with the sharpened back end of the brush. Now, since the digital revolution, instead of drawing on cel I sometimes use a brush-pen on paper, but you don't get the same fluidity on paper. The nearest equivalent that I have found to using a brush on cel is in fact drawing in Flash with the brush tool, which I do a lot."

Paul Vester was born in Cambridge, UK, in 1941 and was brought up in London. He is a filmmaker, animator, and installation artist. He studied at Central Saint Martins College of Art and Design and the Royal College of Art in London, after which he worked as a designer, animator, and director for several London production companies. In 1972 he established his own production company, Speedy Films. Speedy was first built on a series of short animations for Yorkshire Television, followed by a run of French TV commercials, in partnership with Christian Gandon Productions in Paris, which financed his film *Sunbeam* (1980). Speedy produced many British and American TV commercials, which won numerous awards and financed Vester's film *Picnic* (1987). With *Abductees* (1995), he was an early pioneer of the animated documentary form. In 1997 he closed Speedy to move to Los Angeles. He was awarded a Guggenheim Fellowship for his film *In the Woods* (2008). From 2006 to 2011 he co-directed the Experimental Animation program at CalArts, Valencia, California. Vester currently lives and works in Los Angeles and teaches at CalArts.

OPPOSITE Concept drawing for *Sunbeam* credit sequence. Watercolor (6 x 3½")
ABOVE *"The left-hand character is a portrait of one of my sons."* Watercolor (3 x 2½")

ABOVE Drawing, concerning a family drama, made in France. Watercolor
(9¾ x 8")

OPPOSITE Drawing made in Spain. Watercolor (4 x 6")

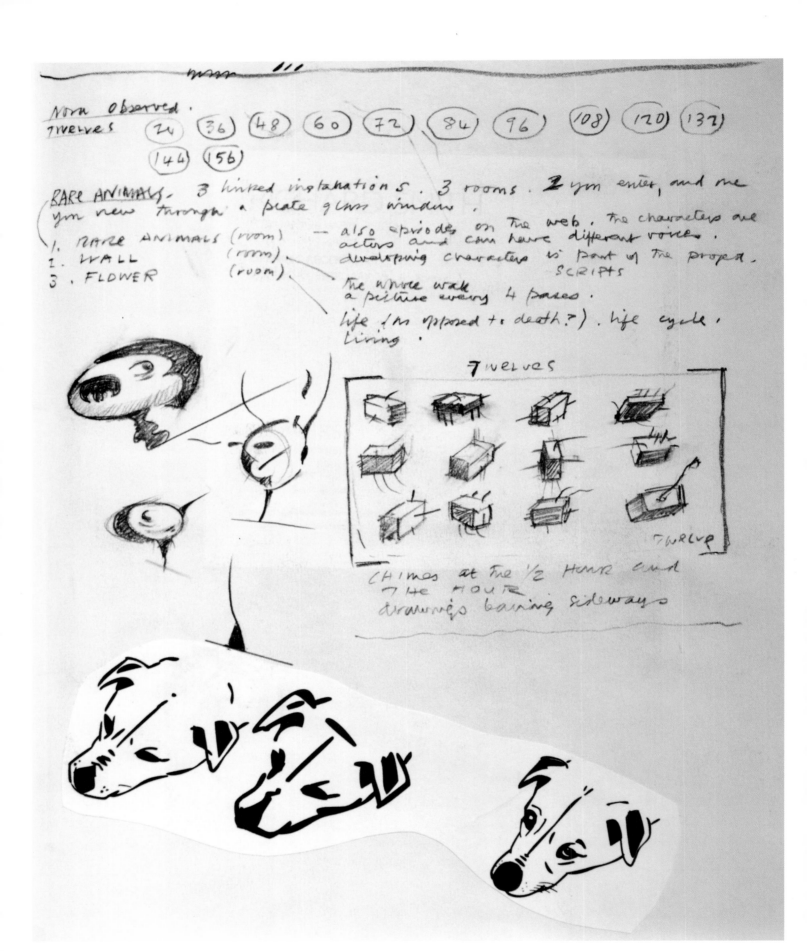

Nora Observed.
Twelves   ⟨24⟩ ⟨36⟩ ⟨48⟩ ⟨60⟩ ⟨72⟩ ⟨84⟩ ⟨96⟩ ⟨108⟩ ⟨120⟩ ⟨132⟩
    ⟨144⟩ ⟨156⟩

RARE ANIMALS. 3 linked installations. 3 rooms. 2 you enter, and one
you view through a plate glass window.

1. RARE ANIMALS (room)   — also episodes on the web. the characters are
2. WALL   (room)   actors and can have different voices.
3. FLOWER   (room)   developing characters is part of the project.
                                        SCRIPTS

                              The whole walk
                              a picture every 4 paces.

                              life (as opposed to death?). life cycle.
                              Living.

                                    TWELVES

CHIMES AT THE ½ HOUR and
THE HOUR
drawings baring sideways

Notes for several projects, including the initial sketch for the *Twelves* installation

Picnic scene 20: panning cel, photographic print, airbrush, cel-vinyl paint (22 x 10")

JJ VILLARD

"I like grease from my chorizo nachos to get on my pages, I like my sketchbook. It's always on me...I draw anytime, anywhere! Like Travis Bickle (DeNiro), driving a taxi! 'ANYTIME, ANYWHERE.'"

J J Villard won a 2nd grade art collage contest in his elementary school and graduated from CalArts, Valencia, California with a BFA in Character Animation. His film *Son of Satan* (2004), which is based on a Charles Bukowski short story, screened at Cannes Film Festival; Museum of Contemporary Art, Los Angeles; Museum of Modern Art, Paris; and at many other film festivals. From CalArts, Villard went directly to DreamWorks Animation, and worked on *Shrek 3, Monsters vs Aliens, Shrek 4, Roadside Attractions,* and *Peabody and Sherman.* He left DreamWorks in 2009 and is currently at Cartoon Network/Adult Swim working on many shows, including his own TV show with Adult Swim "KING STAR KING!"

Drawings from the film *Son of Satan,* 2004

"I don't like showing my sketchbook to many people—unless it is a dirty drawing. I laugh at their reaction. My book has lots of personal and perverted ideas. I get scared people will steal them. It's a silly fear, but I'm never shy in saying 'WHAT THE FUCK ARE U LOOKING AT?' if someone is flipping the pages of my sketchbook."

HIGHWIRE

THE HOWL OF POWER
ERRRR - WHIRRRRRR!

ORDER # DN46448

FEB-12
-DW
WIZARD DISNEY
WEALTH ADULT SWIM
CAN BE SKETCHBOOK
WONDERFUL COMIC
BUT YOU BARPRD
SUCCESS SELF-PORTRAIT
ONE'S MEGILLE RIGHT SYNOPSIS
SURELY AS THE SWAN TEST
STRANGEST AS THE
ADVERSARY

PRIEST: WHAT DO YOU SEE?
CONAN:
UM.... INFINITY.

KINGOSRIC:
WHAT DARING! WHAT
OUTRAGEOUSNESS! WHAT
INSOLENCE! WHAT
ARROGANCE! - I SALUTE YOU.

CHEL WHITE

"In the early to mid-1990s I did a lot of experimentation with what I call 'direct Xerox.' At the time I thought of them as sketches. I kept some of them in a notebook and made notes that would inform my further experiments. The variables I kept track of included fast vs. slow movement (blur vs. no blur), moving with or against the scanner (stretching or compressing), distance from the glass surface (sharp focus or softer focus), etc.

Since the year 2000 my 'sketchbook' has been digital. The cut-out collage aesthetic in my early work, such as Machine Song and Choreography for Copy Machine, carries over into the digital realm. I discovered working this way ultimately provides much more flexibility than working with glue, scissors, and bits of paper, although even today much of my source material still originates as paper. For my digital collage sketches I work almost exclusively in Photoshop. It's more fluid and a lot faster than doing it all by hand, but most of the same rules of composition and aesthetics apply. It's still a process of experimenting with layering, size, color, and composition, but working digitally feels more immediate, more improvisational, and frankly more exciting."

Chel White was born in Kansas City, Missouri, in 1959. Described as a cinematic poet, he sites dreams and the subconscious as his greatest influences. His work has been exhibited at the Museum of Modern Art, New York; the Smithsonian Museum; the Brooklyn Museum, New York; and the Portland Art Museum, New York. He is the recipient of a Rockefeller/Ford Foundation Media Arts Fellowship. His films have screened at festivals such as Berlin, Cannes, Tribeca, SXSW in Austin, Rotterdam, Hiroshima, Annecy, and the Sundance Film Festival. He was awarded Best Short Film at the Stockholm International Film Festival, Best Animated Short at the Florida Film Festival, and Best Narrative Feature at the 2012 Kansas City Film Festival for his debut feature film *Bucksville* (2011), which is about a secret society in the Pacific Northwest.

Harrowdown Hill, White's groundbreaking music video for Radiohead's Thom Yorke, won Best Music Video at the 2007 SXSW Festival. He directed a pair of comedy shorts for NBC's *Saturday Night Live* as well as animated holiday specials for Hallmark. His recent project, *Bird of Flames*, is an experimental music video for David Lynch and Chrysta Bell which straddles the line between stop-motion and live-action. It premiered at the 2012 Cannes International Film Festival as part of the Short Film Corner. His other films include *Choreography for Copy Machine* (1991), Dirt (1998), *Magda* (2004), *A Painful Glimpse into My Writing Process* (2005), and Wind (2007). White lives in Portland, Oregon, where he is a co-founding partner of the film studio Bent Image Lab.

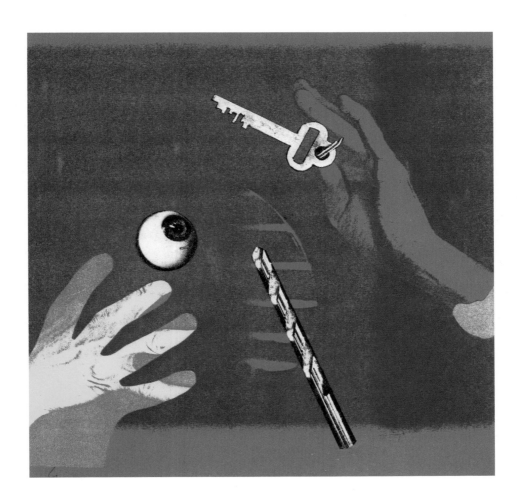

OPPOSITE Direct Xerox collage sketch from *Choreography for Copy Machine* (Photocopy Cha Cha)
ABOVE Direct Xerox sketch from the mid-1990s

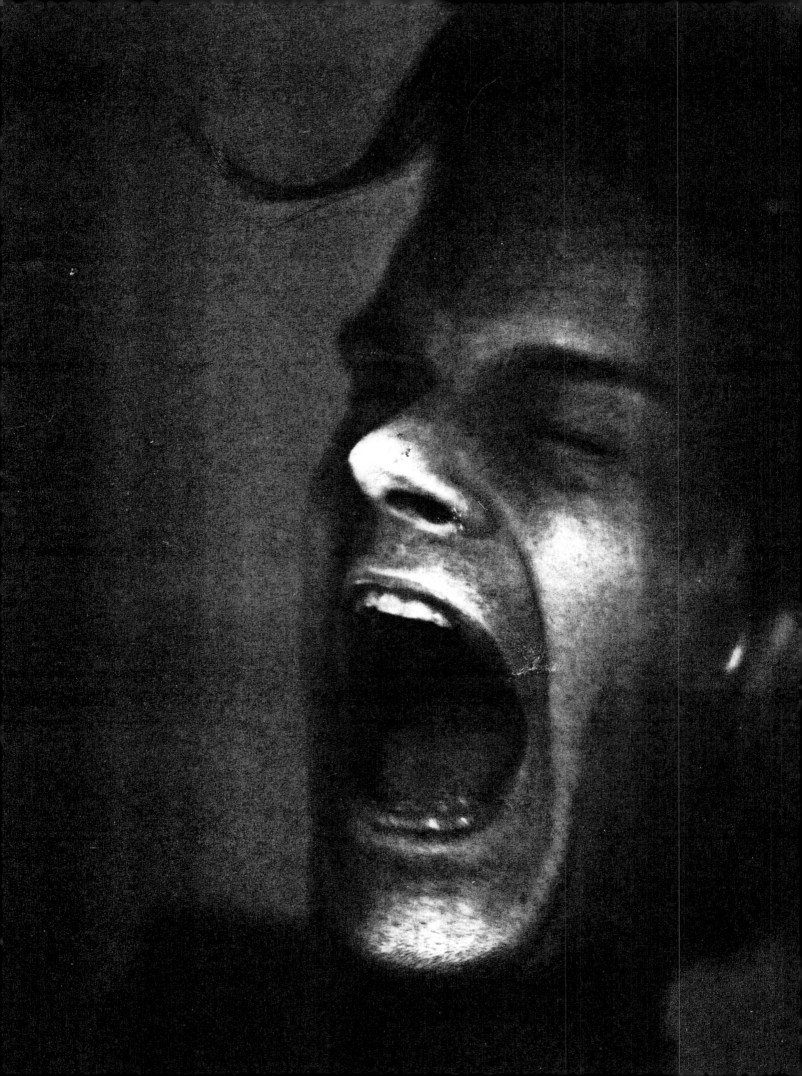

*"I'm fascinated by how different people take to being xeroxed.
I look for the balance between expression and mechanics."*

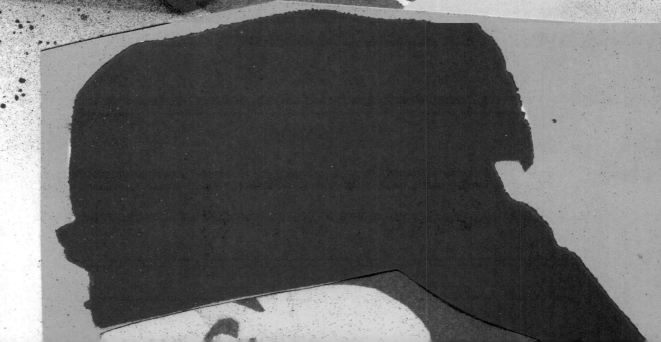

RUN WRAKE

"A sketchbook for me is the place where ideas are born and developed, where I am free to make images that don't need to be anything other than part of a process. The aesthetic quality of sketches is secondary, possessing opposite requirements of a finished piece. I don't really have a process, so a lot of things go in there... It can be a place to get things fantastically wrong—away from prying eyes—a place to stick bits of ephemera that catch the eye, scrawl down the name of a great tune, or even write a shopping list."

Run Wrake began experimenting with animation while studying graphic design at the Chelsea School of Art and Design, London. He went on to gain a master's degree in Animation at the Royal College of Art, London. His graduate film, *Anyway* (1990), received awards in Chicago, Mumbai, London, and from BBC2's "First Bite" competition. Since graduating he has freelanced as an animation director and illustrator, working on a wide variety of projects such as short films, promos, television graphics, commercials, live visuals, and illustration. Highlights include *Jukebox* (1994), working with Howie B, initially on a short film to accompany the release of his album, *Music for Babies,* and subsequently on a series of freeform promos; he has presented storyboards to Roy Lichtenstein for U2's *PopMart Tour*; and his short film *Rabbit* (2005) has received much critical acclaim. Based in rural Kent, UK, he was developing an animated feature film when he passed away in 2012.

OPPOSITE Sketchbook tests for "Angels Go Bald Too," a music video for Howie B, 1997 ABOVE Early Meatheads ready to be color-photocopied, cut out and artworked for the animation that launched M2 in Europe, 1998

perhaps after first hearing of single
and resulting change in outlook, over
next minute or so weirdness fades

Interiors in colour b/gs
(colour Xerox)

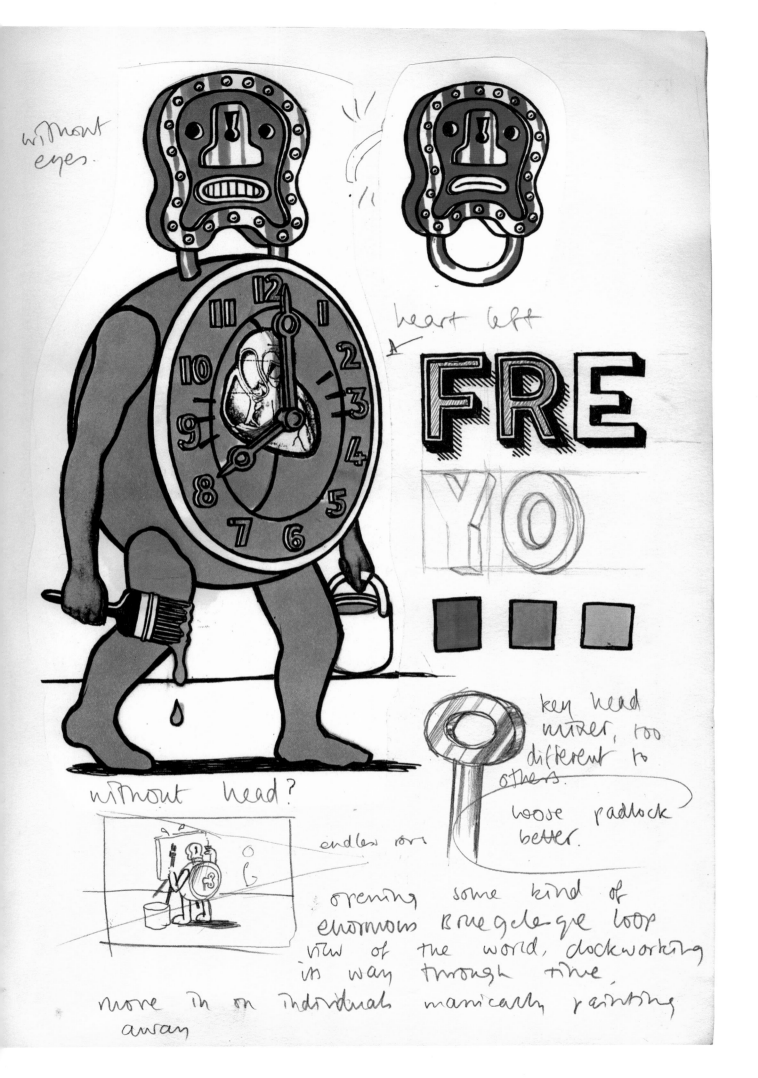

without
eyes.

heart left

FRE
YO

without head?

endless row

key head
mixer, too
different to
others.
loose padlock
better.

opening some kind of
enormous Brueghel-qe loop
view of the world, clockworking
its way through time.
move in on individuals manically painting
away

"Ideas can be born and die within a page. Others can run through book after book, perhaps never to come out of the sketchbook and into the world."

ABOVE Film stills from *Rabbit*, 2005

OPPOSITE Sketchbook page for a music video pitch, "If God Will Send His Angels," U2, 1997

PAGE 308 Sketchbook page for *Jukebox*, 1993

PAGE 309 Sketches for the "Free Your Mind" competition, MTV, 1994

CRAB CANON

10.19.2002. Koji Kimura, Sydney

KOJI YAMAMURA

"My ideas start in my sketchbook. I think small sketches inspire my creative process best. I cut out the ones I like and put them up on the wall of my atelier when making a film. Seeing the drawings while I'm working keeps the idea of the film fresh. My sketchbook is mostly for myself, but I select some pieces for exhibitions and books."

Koji Yamamura was born in Nagoya, Japan, in 1964. He made his first short while still a teenager. He studied at Tokyo Zokei University, where he discovered the work of Ishu Patel, Yuri Norstein, and Priit Pärn. The influence of these masters of animation is apparent in his early films, *Aquatic* (1987), *Japanese-English Pictionary* (1989), and *Perspektivenbox* (1989). During the 1990s Yamamura refined his style, spending much of his time making films

for children: *Kid's Castle* (1995) and *Bavel's Book* (1996). This period culminated in *Your Choice!* (1999), which he made with materials collected from children's animation workshops. *Mt. Head* (*Atama Yama*, 2002) increased Yamamura's visibility after it won the grand prize at the Annecy, Hiroshima, and Zagreb animation festivals; it was also nominated for an Oscar for Best Animated Short. His subsequent productions consolidated his reputation: *The Old Crocodile* (2005), *A Child's Metaphysics* (2007), and especially *Franz Kafka's A Country Doctor* (2007). His 2011 film *Muybridge's Strings* was his first collaboration with the National Film Board of Canada. Since 2008, he has been a professor at the Tokyo University of the Arts in the Department of Animation, Graduate School of Film and New Media.

OPPOSITE Sketchbook drawing for *Muybridge's Strings* ABOVE Film still from *Muybridge's Strings*, 2011
PAGES 314–15 Sketches for *Muybridge's Strings*

"I often draw on the train. Inspiration comes while moving."

ABOVE Film stills from *Muybridge's Strings*, 2011 OPPOSITE Sketchbook drawing for *Muybridge's Strings*

WEBSITES

Nancy Andrews
www.nancyandrews.net

Lilli Carré
www.lillicarre.com

Martha Colburn
www.marthacolburn.com

Luis Cook
www.pearcesisters.co.uk
www.aardman.com

Suzanne Deakin
www.suzannedeakin.com

Jo Dery
www.jodery.com

Paul Driessen
www.pdriessen.com

Félix Dufour-Laperrière
www.felixdl.com

Adam Elliot
www.adamelliot.com.au

Janie Geiser
www.janiegeiser.com

Pierre-Luc Granjon
pierrelucgranjon.blogspot.com

Brent Green
www.nervousfilms.com

Laura Heit
www.lauraheit.com

Don Hertzfeldt
www.bitterfilms.com

Chris Hinton
www.nfb.ca

Jonathan Hodgson
www.hodgsonfilms.com

Stephen Irwin
www.smalltimeinc.com

Avish Khebrehzadeh
www.avishkz.com

Fran Krause
www.frankrause.com

Raimund Krumme
www.acmefilmworks.com

Simone Massi
www.simonemassi.it

Miwa Matreyek
www.semihemisphere.com

Mirai Mizue
www.calf.jp

David OReilly
www.davidoreilly.com

Osbert Parker
www.osbertparker.com

Priit Pärn
www.joonisfilm.ee

Michaela Pavlátová
www.michaelapavlatova.com

Regina Pessoa
www.ciclopefilmes.com

David Polonsky
www.dpolonsky.com

Jeff Scher
www.fezfilms.net

Allison Schulnik
www.allisonschulnik.com

Georges Schwizgebel
www.studio-gds.ch
www.nfb.ca

Maureen Selwood
www.maureenselwood.com

Dash Shaw
www.ruinedcast.com

David Shrigley
www.davidshrigley.com

Cat Solen
www.catsolen.com

Stacey Steers
www.staceysteers.com

Steven Subotnick
www.stevensubotnick.com

Chris Sullivan
www.vimeo.com/sullivananimation

Malcolm Sutherland
www.animalcolm.com

Jim Trainor
www.vdb.org

Ree Treweek
www.theblackheartgang.com
www.shythesun.tv

Paul Vester
www.paulvester.com

J J Villard
www.jjvillard.com
www. facebook.com/jjvillard
twitter.com/jjvillard

Chel White
www.skysociety.com

Run Wrake
www.runwrake.com

Koji Yamamura
www.yamamura-animation.jp

ILLUSTRATION CREDITS

Illustrations in the introduction

fig. 1 Isabel Herguera, drawing from a trip to India
fig. 2 Luis Cook
fig. 3 Malcolm Sutherland, *The Astronomer's Dream* storyboard
fig. 4 Malcolm Sutherland, *Astronaut's Dream* storyboard
fig. 5 Don Hertzfeldt, camera notes
fig. 6 Priit Pärn, character study for *Karl and Marilyn*
fig. 7 Koji Yamamura, hand study for *Franz Kafka's A Country Doctor*
fig. 8 Michaela Pavlátová
fig. 9 Martha Colburn
fig. 10 Malcolm Sutherland
fig. 11 J J Villard

Illustrations by page number

12 © 2009 Nancy Andrews
30 © 2009 Martha Colburn
35 © 2007 Aardman Animations
47 © 2000 Jo Dery
49 below, left and below, right © 2005 Jo Dery
52-53 © 2004 ONF/NFB CinéTé Filmproductie bv
54-55 © 2000 ONF/NFB
60-61 © 2008 Folimage-ONF/NFB-Noir Blanc Animation-ARTE France
62 © 2009 Melodorama Pictures
69 © 1994 Janie Geiser
85 © 2006 Brent Green/Nervous Films
87 © 2005 Slinky Pictures/Maria Manton/Laura Heit
88 above and below © 2011 Laura Heit
97 © 2010 Isabel Herguera
98, 102 above, 103 above © 2008 Don Hertzfeldt
102 below, 103 below © 2011 Don Hertzfeldt
104-109 Steve Hillenburg Sketches © 2012 United Plankton Productions, Inc. All Rights Reserved.
115 © 2011 Jonathan Hodgson/Sherbet/BBC
119 © 2011 Stephen Irwin
120 © 2010 Stephen Irwin
124 © 2007 Avish Khebrehzadeh
128-29 © 2011 Avish Khebrehzadeh
147 © 2009 Sacrebleu Productions/ Simone Massi
148 © 2010 Miwa Matreyek
152-53 © 2007 Miwa Matreyek
158-59 © 2006 Les Films de l'Arlequin, ONF/NFB, Arte France
166 © 2010 David OReilly
173 © 2007 Osbert Parker
177 © 2006 Osbert Parker
178, 184-85 © 2008 Priit Pärn and Olga Pärn
179 © 2007 Priit Pärn
180-81, 182-83 © 2002 Priit Pärn
189 © 2011 Sacrebleu/Negativ productions
196 © 2005 Folimage, Ciclope Filmes, ONF/NFB and Arte France
198-99 © 2012 Folimage, Ciclope Filmes, ONF/NFB, Studio GDS, Arte France and RTS (Radio Television Suisse)
205 above and below © 2008 Bridgit Folman Film Gang
207 © 2007 Jeff Scher
217 © 2011 Allison Schulnik
222-23 © 2011 ONF/NFB, Studio GDS, Radio Television Suisse
225, 229 © 2009 Maureen Selwood
226-27 © 2012 Maureen Selwood
238, 240-41 © 2006 David Shrigley
249, 250, below, 252 © 2011 Stacey Steers
258-59 © 2009 Steven Subotnick

264 © 2012 Chris Sullivan
270 above and below © 2009 Malcolm Sutherland
275, 278 © 2008 Jim Trainor
283 © 2006 The Black Heart Gang
294-95 © 2003 J J Villard
310 © 2005 Run Wrake
313, 316 © 2011 ONF/NFB/NHK/ Polygon Pictures

ACKNOWLEDGMENTS

First of all, I want to thank the 51 artists included in this book for their work and time—all of whom generously allowed me, and now you, to peek into their sketchbooks and shuffle through their piles. This book wouldn't exist without their unique visions and passionate scrawlings. It was such a pleasure working with all of you.

I want to thank my editor Andrew Sanigar for inviting me to make the book I'd often thought about, and for his guidance in the process of creating my first book.

Thank you to Victoria Forrest for the wonderful design and layout.

Thank you to Ryan Goodwin Smith and Blake Young, my editoral assistants on both sides of the pond at different points along the way.

And thank you to my husband Kris whose patience and unwavering support kept the ship afloat.